I0474013

# Wall Street

## The Real Deal

Andrew Lawrence

Name : Wall Street - The Real Deal

ISBN-10 : 1467919500

EAN-13 : 978-1467919500

Printer : CreateSpace

Color : Black/white with No Bleed

Country of Publication : United States

Author : Andrew Lawrence

Cover Design : Andrew Lawrence

# Books by Andrew Lawrence

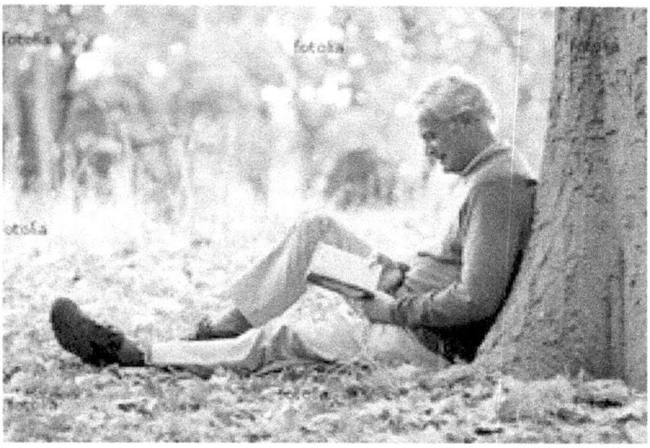

Wall Street - The Real Deal
MONEY - The Basics
The Final Bubble
Glimmers Of Hope
The Happiness Transformation
Discover Your Life Purpose in 30 Minutes
Stories Of A Lifetime
Soul Sex: The Ultimate Pleasure
How To Thrive After 65
Solve Your Customer Service Problem …Fast
Beat Your Fatigue … in 10 Seconds

Available at amazon.com

## AUTHOR'S NOTE

Yes, I could have written a 400-page book about Wall Street but these days no one wants to read 400 pages about ANYTHING. So, instead of writing typical 400-page books I have kept mine short, sweet, easy to read, easy to understand, and real. All 11 of them.

# TABLE OF CONTENTS

## Introduction

I was a Wall Street professional. In New York. For over a decade. A decade on Wall Street is like 25-30 years in a normal job. Being a Wall Street trader is kind of like being a fighter pilot. Or a professional athlete. Or a high-end hooker. Intense, stressful and requiring great talent and skill. I worked for some of the premier Wall Street investment houses, as a money market trader, trading and managing investment and securities portfolios in excess of $400 million. I once got a standing ovation from my colleagues (yes, I was embarrassed).

On Wall Street I learned the fundamentals of the huge American financial system, not from college professors or textbooks or political pundits or from TV news or blogs or from listening to the opinions of friends and family members. I learned it from working at it 12 hours a day in the real world, the real world of high finance, on Wall Street. And I am going to pass that valuable hard-earned knowledge along to you. Wall Street. Wall Street made simple. The real deal. Right here. Right now.

These days I am retired. Now, I sit on my ass and write books. Inspirational self-help books. Books that make you smarter, richer and happier. This is my 11th book. The book is a simple explanation of what Wall Street really is, why it exists, and what it does. And why it is important to y-o-u and your life. It is the real deal. It is a short book, written in plain and simple English, so that the average person, with little or no knowledge of economics or high finance or stocks and bonds, can understand it. The reason I wrote the book is because, over my lifetime, I observed that NOBODY, outside of those working on Wall Street, really understands what Wall Street is and what it does. Everyone has an opinion or a feeling about Wall Street but they have no factual basis or real world experience on which to base it on. We, as Americans, have no true knowledge of what Wall Street is, why it exists, and what it does. We get plenty of opinions about Wall Street from people who don't know what they are talking about or who have a particular political agenda, pro or con, but we never get the real facts, the real and simple Truth, about money and Wall Street. Yet money, and Wall Street, is a critical and fundamental part of life in America. Whether you like it or not.

Read the book. It's simple. And short. And very interesting. And very educational. It's the real deal. Then, after reading it, form your OWN opinion of Wall Street.

Regards,

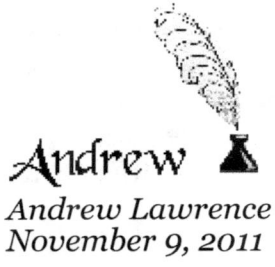

Andrew

*Andrew Lawrence*
*November 9, 2011*

# Chapter 1 **Wall Street - A Very Brief History**

*Wall Street 1867*

According to hermes-press.com … "In the 17th century, Dutch settlers had built a wall at the foot of New York Harbor to protect themselves from Indians, pirates, and other dangers. The path near the wall had become a bustling commercial thoroughfare because it joined the banks of the East River with those of the Hudson River on the west. The path was named Wall Street. Early merchants built their warehouses and shops on this path, along with a city hall and a church.

New York was the U.S. national capitol from 1785 until 1790 and Federal Hall was built on Wall Street. George Washington, the first President of the United States, was inaugurated on April 30, 1789 on the steps of this building.

In March, 1792, twenty-four of New York City's leading merchants met secretly at Corre's Hotel to discuss ways to bring order to the securities business and to wrest it from their competitors, the auctioneers. Two months later, on May 17, 1792, these merchants signed a document named the Buttonwood Agreement, named after their traditional meeting place; outdoors, under a buttonwood tree.

These twenty-four men had founded what was to become the New York Stock Exchange."

For over 100 years, Wall Street has been the dominant financial center of the world. Today it employs hundreds of thousands of workers and utilizes the latest technology to create and maintain the U.S. financial markets, raise enormous sums of money for business and government, and transfers trillions of dollars of capital and investments ... every day.

# Chapter 2 **Why Wall Street Exists**

The U.S., and the world, needs Wall Street. The U.S., and the world, needs Wall Street for several reasons. Financial reasons. Wall Street is the center of the world, financially speaking. The center of almost everything financial. In New York's financial center, known as Wall Street, municipal governments raise funds for education via issuing bonds, the federal government raises trillions of dollars every year to fund its operations, corporations raise funds; to grow, to expand, to create new products and services and to create jobs, pension funds invest YOUR pension money on Wall Street. Wall Street is the source of capital for the giant U.S. economy and its private and public sectors. Without capital the U.S could never have grown from 13 colonies on the East Coast to 50 states spread out over 2,500 miles wide and 1,500 miles long. Without Wall Street, without the utilization of capital, you would not be living in a country with one of the highest standards of living in the world.

And, from halfwayinteresting.com, "The effects of Wall Street on our community can be found in every corner of life. Your car, produced by a company that used Wall Street money to finance its plants and operations, your purchase/lease financed by a company that packaged and sold your loan to a Wall Street banker to bring in new cash to lend to new car buyers.

Your home, built with products from companies that were funded by Wall Street bankers, financed with a mortgage loan that was funded by Wall Street capital, and powered by a utility whose plant and operations were funded by a Wall Street debt offering. The cable/ satellite TV you watch, their cable lines or satellites were funded by Wall Street investors, your cell phone is from a company that … used Wall Street …investment capital, to fund expansions, acquisitions, and technological upgrades.

Your schools, your roads, the airports, the train system, your retirement, etc, all funded with the … investment capital of Wall Street bankers. There is hardly anything that is a part of our world that hasn't been funded in some way by Wall Street. That is our … American … heritage, the greatest financial system the world has ever known. Capitalism. It has survived good and bad Presidents, awful and courageous Congresses, and excellent and flawed Supreme Court decisions, natural disasters, war, and every calamity that has come our way for over 100 years."

**Simply put, without Wall Street there would be no modern day United States of America. Without Wall Street there would be no "modern" American civilization. And we would likely be living in a hut or a cave ... gathering wood to build a fire … and worrying about hunting, catching or growing our next meal.**

# Chapter 3 **The Fear Of Money**

Before we get deeper into Wall Street let's talk about money. Why? Because Wall Street is based on money. And many people, it seems, have a fear of money. Does the thought of having a lot of money make you uncomfortable? Cause you anxiety? If so, it may be that you are buying into the myths about money. Myths that are simply untrue. In fact, many of the most common statements about money are often misquoted, wrong, or were made by people who did not understand money ... or had none.

Let's look at a few of the myths about money ...

**"Money is the root of all evil"**
Everybody has heard this one. Unfortunately, it's one of the most famous misquotes of all time. The original quote comes from the New Testament and the correct quote is "the LOVE of money is the root of all evil". The love of money is an obsession and thus the true quote warns of the potential corruption that can derive from a love of, or obsession with, money (or any unhealthy preoccupation with ANYTHING). The fact is that money itself is neither good nor evil.

It is neutral. Money can be used for good or it can be used for bad. How it is used is a choice, and the choice of how to use money is in the hands of he (or she) who controls it.

**"Money is Power" (and power corrupts)**
Money itself has no real power. For instance, if you were legally given 10 million after-tax dollars in cash, put it in a safe deposit box, never touched it and never told anyone you had it you would have no more power than you do right now. The power of money comes from the use (or misuse) of it or the perceived benefit or threat by others. The money itself does not generate any power; it has to be converted into power. And whether or not you wish to convert money into power is a choice. And if one decides to convert money into power that power may be used for good or for evil, depending on the character of the person with the money.

**"Money will change your life"**
Let's hope so! Used wisely, money can greatly ease many of life's burdens and greatly enhance one's life. Or, if you have a weak character, choose to live in fear and worry, you can let money make you miserable. It's not the money, it's YOU. The important thing to realize is that you get to control the money, it doesn't get to control you. Want proof? Here's how much actual control you have over your money - in the extreme, you can always give all your money away - and be rid of it. Just like that. You can give it all to charity, you can throw it out the window, you can walk down the street and hand it out. You can give it all away. It's your money and you can do whatever you want with it, including give it away. Gone. You can make it all disappear if you choose to do so. That may be a stupid choice but that choice is always yours. That's the ultimate power you have over your money and it rests in your hands. Money doesn't ruin or change your life or change you or take control over your life. Unless you let it. And since you have the ultimate power to get rid of it why would you let it run, or ruin, your life?

**"Money can't buy you happiness"**
This is true - if you are not happy to begin with. However, if you reasonably well-adjusted, have a good value system and a little control over yourself money won't hurt you either. Contrary to popular wisdom, money and happiness are not mutually exclusive. In fact, money can greatly enhance the security, independence and well being of your life, your family's life and the lives of people you care about. Money can't buy you happiness but happiness can't buy you money!

To sum it up, the fear of money is often based on misconceptions. The truth is that money itself is simply an inanimate object, doesn't know or care who does what with it, has no moral or ethical value itself and is a necessary commodity to have in the civilized world. Money, in the hands of whoever has it, has the capacity for great good or great evil, depending on who is doing the spending. It is not money that should be judged but the character and actions of the person (or entity) who uses it.

Money is nothing to fear.

OK, now that you have no fear of money let's learn more about Wall Street …

# Chapter 4 **What is Wall Street?**

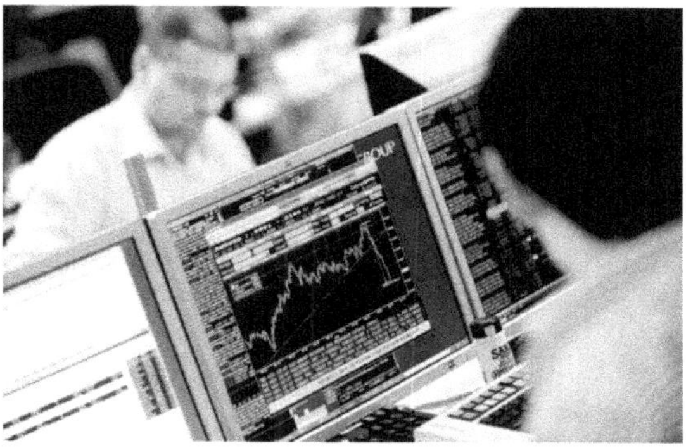

Wall Street is actually an "umbrella" term for many and varied financial markets, centered in New York. Wall Street markets include many different financial markets, financial services and financial securities. Here is a simple, brief and interesting explanation of the major securities markets centered on Wall Street …

**The stock market**

According to wikipedia, "There is little consensus among scholars as to when corporate stock was first traded. Some see the key event as the Dutch East India Company's founding in 1602, while others point to earlier developments."

According to Thinkquest.org, during the American Revolution "… the first of the nation's banks started to sell parts or shares of their own companies to people in order to raise money. In essence they sold off part of the company to whomever wanted to buy it, which is the essence of the modern day stock market. The 1900s brought the Industrial Revolution, and along with it, a boom in Wall Street. Everybody wanted a piece of the action, and Wall Street grew. The New York Stock Exchange was not the only way to buy stocks at that time. Many stocks that were deemed not good enough for the NYSE, were traded outside on the curbs. This so called "curb trading," has

now become the American Stock Exchange (AMEX).
Today, the New York and the American Stock Exchanges, have been joined by the NASDAQ, and hundreds of local and international Stock Exchanges, that all play a part in the national and global economy.

**What is a stock?**
A stock is a certificate that shows that you own a small fraction of a corporation. When you buy a stock, you are paying for a small percentage of everything that that company owns, buildings, chairs, computers, etc. When you own a stock, you are referred to as a shareholder or a stockholder. In essence, **a stock is a representation of the amount of a company that you own.** It is a piece of paper. Called a stock certificate.

The benefit of owning stock in a corporation is that whenever the corporation profits, you profit as well. For example, if you buy stock in Coca Cola, and they come out with a new drink that everyone buys in massive quantities, then the company will profit tremendously, and so will you. The value of your shares will go up and, just because you own the stock, your wealth will increase. And owning a share of stock also gives you the right to make decisions that may influence the company. Each share of stock you own has a little bit of voting power, so the more shares you own, the more decision making power you have as a voting shareholder.

**Why the stock market exists**
Here is a good and simple explanation from about.com of why the stock market exists …

"Business is the cornerstone of … our … economy. Almost every large corporation started out as a small, mom-and-pop operation and through growth, became financial giants. Wal-Mart, Dell Computer, and McDonald's had combined profits of $10.34 billion this year. Wal-Mart was originally a single-store business in Arkansas. Dell computer began with Michael Dell selling computers out of his college dorm room. McDonald's was once a small restaurant no one had heard of. How did these small companies grow from tiny, hometown enterprises to three of the largest businesses in the American economy? They raised capital by selling stock in themselves. When a company is growing, the biggest hurdle is often raising enough money to expand. Owners generally have two options to overcome this. They can either borrow the money from a bank or venture capitalist, or sell part of the business to investors and use the money to fund growth. Taking out a loan is common, and very useful – to a point. Banks will not always lend money to … young … companies … and there are other financial and control factors. Factors … that … often provoke owners of small businesses to issue stock. In exchange for giving up a … fraction of control, they are given cash to expand the business … (and create j-o-b-s). In addition to money that doesn't have to be paid back … like a bank loan … "going public" [as its called when a company sells stock in itself for the first time]" … is often the best choice for a company and its owners." It's also a good way for the company's owner to become an instant millionaire or billionaire!

Investopedia gives a good explanation of what the stock market does: "The purpose of a stock market is to facilitate the exchange of securities (equity shares, i.e. ownership shares) between buyers and sellers, reducing the risks of investing. Just imagine how difficult it would be to sell shares if you had to call around the neighborhood trying to find a buyer. Really, a stock market is nothing more than a super-sophisticated farmers' market linking buyers and sellers."
Thinkquest.org raises, and answers, an interesting question: "Some of you might be wondering why should you care about the stock market. Maybe you are too young to be investing, or can't see how the market relates to your every day life. The fact is, even if you have no money in the stock market, or are in school, the stock market does affect you. It affects everything you do, from going to the mall, to buying that new outfit you have always wanted. After all, clothing designer Calvin Klein has to get money to make those outfits!" And if

you work, and have a pension, your pension money is often invested for you. In the stock market. Through Wall Street. When the stock market goes up, the value of your pension goes up. If the stock market goes down, the value of your pension goes down. That is a strong and important connection between Main St and Wall St. Wall St is where YOUR retirement pension is. That's where EVERYONE'S retirement pension is in America. That is why Main St should care - a lot - about Wall St.

**The bond market**

Which is bigger, the stock market or the bond market?

**Bond market vs stock market**

Average daily trading volume (2009)
U.S. stock market: $105 billion
U.S. bond market: $814 billion

Nearly a trillion dollars worth of bonds are traded every day! A trillion is 1,000 billions. Here is what 1 trillion dollars looks like …

*One trillion dollars, stacked next to a tractor trailer and a person*

The bond market provides local, state and federal governments, and private enterprises the funds needed to get development and long-term infrastructure projects off the ground. Before people are hired, earth moved, concrete poured, or products rolled off the factory floor, capital needed for the work is in place. Chances are bond issues helped raise the funds to get started on projects that help maintain our quality of life, well-being and U.S. competitiveness.

The issuance and purchase of bonds help lower costs of infrastructure renovation and replacement for public works, as well as for new and expanding businesses. Among many examples, bonds help build bridges, roads, transportation systems, power plants that light and heat our homes, reservoirs and pipes that bring us water, sewer systems and factories that produce products fundamental to our daily lives. Without bonds to finance these projects in a timely way, these systems would erode and break down. By the end of 2010, issuance in the U.S. bond markets had reached $6.7 trillion.

In addition to financing long-term infrastructure projects, bonds help governments manage the ebb of its cash flow … and … help the government pay for needed services, such as those provided by military, police, hospital staff, school teachers, and others.

**Government bond market**

According to wikipedia, "In 1171, the authorities of the Republic of Venice, concerned about their war-depleted treasury, drew a forced loan from the citizenry. Such debt, known as prestiti, paid 5 percent interest per year and had an indefinite maturity date. Initially regarded with suspicion, it came to be seen as a valuable investment that could be bought and sold. The government bond market had begun. In the middle of the 13th century, bankers in Venice, Italy began to trade in government securities. In 1351 the Venetian government outlawed spreading rumors intended to lower the price of government funds. Bankers in Pisa and Florence also began trading in government securities during the 14th century."

The U.S. government securities market started much later. According to the U.S. Treasury Department, "The history of the Department of the Treasury began in the turmoil of the American Revolution, when the Continental Congress at Philadelphia deliberated the crucial issue of financing a war of independence against Great Britain. The Congress had no power to levy and collect taxes, nor was there a tangible basis for securing funds from foreign investors or governments. The delegates resolved to issue paper money in the form of bills of credit, promising redemption in coin on faith in the revolutionary cause. On June 22, 1775 -- only a few days after the Battle of Bunker Hill, Congress issued $2 million in bills." The first U.S. Treasury securities.

Today, U.S. Treasuries, debt securities issued by the Department of the Treasury on behalf of the Federal government, carry the full faith and credit backing of the U.S. government, making it the safest and most popular of investments.

The liquidity and efficiency of the Treasury market, via Wall Street, allows the federal government to finance ongoing operations in an efficient way at the lowest possible cost to taxpayers over time.

The amount of marketable U.S. Treasury securities is huge, with $8.85 trillion in outstanding bills, notes, and bonds as of the end of 2010. Trading volume in Treasury securities averaged $949.8 billion a day in 2010.

**Municipal Bond Market**

Tens of thousands of state and local governments issue bonds to build, repair and improve schools, streets, hospitals, airports and many other public works. Encompassing a diverse group, municipal bonds, popularly called "munis" on average traded a daily $15.0 billion in 2010, totaling some 41,643 trades a day. Municipal bonds, as a whole, are among the least risky of investments.

**Corporate Bond Market**

Corporations use the funds they raise from selling bonds for a variety of purposes, from building facilities to purchasing equipment to expanding their business. The U.S. corporate bond market is large and liquid, with daily trading volume estimated at $16.3 billion. Issuance for 2010 was an estimated $1.03 trillion. Outstanding corporate debt stands at $7.5 trillion in 2010. The U.S. corporate bond markets have long been an important source of capital for corporations who issue them. Early IOUs or debt obligations financed the country's westward expansion, building the transcontinental railroad and Erie Canal.

**Money Market Instruments**

While governments and corporations typically tap the securities markets for long-term funding needs, they may also need to issue debt for shorter periods to finance imports, to meet seasonal cash-flow needs or to create "bridge" financing until conditions are right for longer-term debt issues. To obtain this type of safe short-term financing (maturities of one year or less), they can turn to the "money market," which includes bankers' acceptances, commercial paper and certificates of deposit (CDs) and short term Treasury bills. Additionally, the money market's efficiency, liquidity and size, estimated currently at $2.86 trillion, frequently make these instruments cost-effective alternative funding sources relative to bank loans. From the investor's perspective, money market instruments represent a liquid, low-risk investment that generally offers a higher yield than bank deposits. Mutual funds and other large investors are the principal investors in money market instruments.

# Chapter 5 **Banks vs. Investment Banking**

There are banks and then there are investment banks. In its simplest terms here are the major differences between commercial banks and Wall Street investment banks:

A regular commercial bank usually has neighborhood branches, is open to the public, accepts deposits from individuals, offers checking and savings accounts, atms, makes mortgage loans and auto loans and larger banks often issue credit cards.

Investment banks do none of these things. An investment bank does not do business with the public but rather offers its many services to institutions; local, state and federal government and corporations. Investment banking historically has been the business of "high" finance; mergers and acquisitions, advising corporations as to financing, private funding, taking a company public in an Initial Public Offering (IPO), underwriting and trading of stocks, bonds and other securities. Investment banks and brokerage firms dominate the world of Wall St. Banks do not. Investment banking is a world away from normal commercial banking.

According to small business.chron.com, “The banking sector is split into two fundamental divisions: investment banking and commercial banking.

**Risk Tolerance**

Investment banks have a higher risk tolerance due to their business model and the relative weakness of government regulation in the industry. Commercial banks are much less tolerant of risk. Panic can ensue if families and businesses lose their checking and savings accounts, so commercial banks have an implied fiduciary duty to act in the best interest of their clients, not to mention the tight strings attached to commercial banks. Deposits in commercial banks are often covered by FDIC insurance.”

According to about.com,

**Activities of a Typical Investment Bank**

A typical investment bank will engage in some or all of the following activities:

- Raise equity capital (e.g., helping launch an IPO or creating a special class of stock that can be placed with sophisticated investors such as insurance companies or banks)
- Raise debt capital (e.g., issuing bonds to help raise money for a factory expansion)
- Insure bonds or launching new financial products
- Engage in proprietary trading where teams of in-house money managers invests or trades the company’s own money for its private account

Some large banks also function as investment banking companies.

The top 10 investment banks in 2010 were …

1. J.P. Morgan - earned fees of $5.5 billion
2. Bank of America Merrill Lynch - earned fees of $4.5 billion
3. Goldman Sachs - earned fees of $4.3 billion
4. Morgan Stanley - earned fees of 4.0 billion
5. Credit Suisse (Switzerland) - earned fees of $3.3 billion
6. Deutsche Bank (Germany) - earned fees of $3.2 billion
7. Citi Group (U.S.) - earned fees of $3.2 billion
8. Barclay's Capital (UK) - earned fees of $2.8 billion
9. UBS (Switzerland) - earned fees of $2.6 billion
10. BNP Paribus (France) - earned fees of $1.4 billion

# Chapter 6 **It's all About the Money**

Money. "Money makes the world go 'round". We've all heard about money; the good, the bad and the ugly. But what is the actual purpose of money? The purpose of money is: convenience. Money is lightweight, portable, easy to transport and can even be transferred electronically. Money can be used to purchase every kind of product or service a person might want or need. Money makes trade and commerce, between individuals and between nations, faster and more efficient.

Money is the standard of measuring wealth. All wealth is denominated in terms of money. Even hard assets (tangible assets) such as real estate and natural resources like oil, gold, diamonds, etc. are valued based on what they are worth if converted to cash. In today's world (at least in America) money is a basic necessity of life. It's how you get food, shelter, clothing, transportation and all the other basic ingredients of life. It's also how you get rich.

The <u>purpose</u> of money is to conveniently pay for things.

The <u>result</u> of money is financial security.
The <u>point</u> of money is living well.

What's the point of having money if you don't use it to better your life? Or the lives of others? I am not talking about extravagance or opulence (which certainly has its place if you want that) I'm talking about having financial security, and having nice things; a nice house, a nice car, a nice vacation, nice shoes and if you are a woman, nice shoes AND nice handbags. Money can be used to improve your life and your lifestyle. With money you can help family members and friends who need financial help, you can get better healthcare, you can get better dental care, you can get braces for your kids, send your kids to private school (if your local public school is not a good school), you can get a maid to clean your house once or twice a week (or every day), you can pay off all your debts, if you so desire you can get plastic surgery to improve your looks or look younger and, if you're a politician, you can get $400 haircuts.

When you don't have money, or enough money, life can be difficult and, often, not very much fun. Without money you constantly struggle and worry and can feel deprived and resentful. When you have money you don't have to struggle as much, you don't have to worry as much about finances and you don't have to feel deprived and resentful. And, when you have money, you get treated with more respect and you are thought to be more interesting, smarter, and more attractive.

When you have money you can live well. And living well is the best revenge.

Money, however, is not the ultimate goal in life. The ultimate goal in life is happiness. Of course, you can be a lot happier if you have a lot of money!

And, if you do have a lot of money, you can also help others in the world who are less fortunate. If you have a lot of money you can donate some of it to causes you believe in, you can help build schools and hospitals and help fund critical assistance programs in poverty stricken areas of the world. If you have a lot of money you can not only live well but you can also do a lot of good for others. That is the true purpose of money. Unless you are a greedy selfish jerk.

The purpose of money is convenience. What is the purpose of Wall Street? The purpose of Wall Street is finance. High finance. Money. Lots of money. Big money. Huge sums of money. Billions and trillions of dollars to finance industrial growth and government programs. Billions and trillions of dollars. Billions and trillions of dollars that nobody ever sees. The huge sums that trade hands every day on Wall Street are simply numbers, electronic notations, that transfers money from one account to another. It's not like they wheel in a barrel of actual money when a trade is made. They don't. You never see the actual dollars, they just appear as numbers on a computer screen. The first time I had to do a calculation for a trade of 5 million dollars I was overwhelmed. 5 million dollars? I had never seen even $1,000 in actual money in one place before. $5 MILLION? I was freaked out. I could not conceive of that much money in one place. By the end of the week, having done hundreds of calculations for hundreds of $5 million trades, I got used to the big numbers. Because they were only numbers. I got used to dealing in numbers, big numbers, not actual real money. I never saw the actual real money. I only saw the numbers, big numbers but they were only numbers, numbers which represented the billions and trillions of dollars traded on Wall Street. Shortly, five million dollar trades became no longer overwhelming, became simply a 5, six zeros and 2 commas. 5,000,000. It was math, not real money. The money became the math. In the end it's not all about the money - it's all about the math. In reality, if you want the insider's viewpoint, Wall Street is really all about the math, not the money.

# Chapter 7 **Capitalism 101**

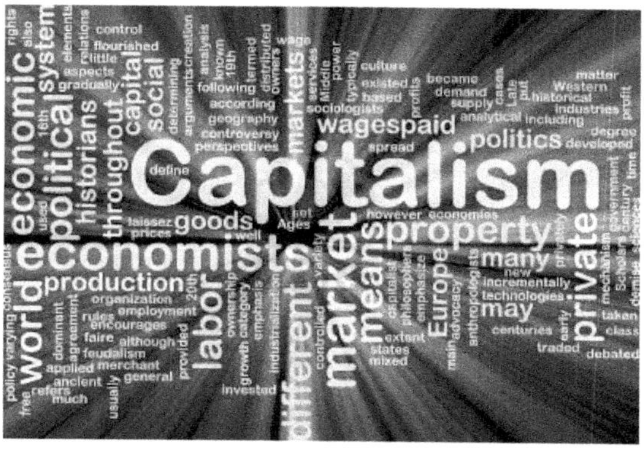


To understand Wall Street, and money, it's important to have a basic understanding of the American economic system. I'll try to make it as interesting and as simple as possible. But first let me digress for moment …

Many Americans today believe that "war is not the answer". They would do well to remember that America was created and founded on a war. A war of independence. A war for freedom. Personal freedom and economic freedom. And from that war came the U.S. Constitution and the Bill of Rights, affording personal and economic freedom and opportunity to all modern day Americans. America is the Great Experiment, breaking many of the world's pre-existing rules and customs. Throughout its history, America has constantly adapted, making new laws and new rules and new customs and new ways of life for its citizens. As a result of the War of Independence, today Americans are free to make life up as they go along, as they see fit, constantly reinventing themselves and their country. That is the true strength and the true secret of America.

Since colonial days, America has been blessed with abundant natural resources, an abundance of land and a pioneering inventive spirit. America flourished from the 1600's through the 1900's. Because America was so huge and had so little population the early American settlers had to rely on themselves for food, shelter and trade. And, as many early settlers were farmers, trappers or traders who lived far outside the cities, often in the middle of nowhere, they had to be self-reliant and self-sufficient in order to survive. And, as necessity is the mother of invention, American pioneers created new and different and efficient ways to survive and prosper. And because, in the wilderness of mountains and the vast prairies and the Old West, laws were difficult to enforce (sometimes judges had to travel hundreds of miles on a circuit to bring law to the settlers), there was little or no infrastructure, travel was by horseback, wagon or on foot, the early American pioneers had to rely mainly on their wits … and their guns.

The early American pioneers and early American cowboys represent the epitome of the American spirit and the epitome of American freedom. This independent, uniquely American spirit carried through well into the 20th century and is the true and main reason for whatever positive impact America has had on society and the world.

<u>The American pioneering spirit is the basis for America's tremendous economic success and the basis for its economic system, capitalism.</u>

According to Wikipedia, "Capitalism is an economic system in which property is owned by private persons and corporations, not government, and operated for profit. In a capitalist economy, investments, distribution, income, production and pricing of goods and services are predominantly determined through the operation of a free market. Capitalism is usually considered to involve the right of individuals and corporations to trade, using money, in goods, services (including finance), labor and land."

Capitalism is derived from the word capital. Capital means "money“. Capitalism is based on money in the hands of individuals and businesses. Money in the hands of individuals and companies with the freedom to use that money as they see fit (within the law). Under capitalism you are free to accumulate money, spend it, invest it or save it as you see fit.

Under capitalism you are free to risk your money by starting your own business. This is called entrepreneurship. Under capitalism, if you risk your money and start a business
and are successful, you are rewarded. Rewarded with more money. If you risk your money and start a business and that business fails you lose all your money. Risk versus reward.

**Starting a business is part of the American dream** America is a nation of small businesses, a nation of entrepreneurs. Many men and women in the U.S. dream of being their own boss. Why? Because, as an employee, they can't stand the politics and the rigidity and the stupidity that exists in bigger companies and in government. And many people want more control over their own work, over their future, their destiny, and they want to be able to do things their way, not someone else's way. They want freedom and independence. How prevalent is this American dream? 71% of teenagers say they are interested in becoming entrepreneurs.

The American economy is driven by entrepreneurs and small business. Small business is also where the jobs are. Most employees in the U.S. do not work for giant corporations
or for the government; they work in small businesses (under 100 employees). Small businesses provide 60%-80% of all new jobs in a given year.

**Who do YOU work for?**

___ government, union or non-profit
___ large corporation
___ small business
___ yourself

___ retired
___ stay-at-home mom (or dad)
___ unemployed
___ student
___ independently wealthy and don't need to work

**Why small business is important**

In its simplest form, when a small business grows it does more business and expands, by hiring more employees. When the small business grows even more it has to hire even more employees to handle the increase in business. More employees means more jobs for more people. More jobs means more employees; more people getting paid and making more money. And what do employees do with the money they earn? They spend it on goods and services they need and want. When Americans earn more money they tend to spend more money, and tend to raise their standard of living and their lifestyle. This is called consumer spending.

**Consumer spending**

Consumer spending accounts for 2/3rds of the entire U.S. economy. Consumer spending is based on people having money and spending it. Having money to spend is largely based on having a job. When more people have jobs and incomes (or higher incomes), overall spending in the economy goes up. When consumer spending goes up the economy is "good". When people lose their jobs they lose their income and spend less; causing overall consumer spending in the economy to go down and the economy becomes a "bad" economy. It's all pretty simple, it's all about jobs and income and consumer spending.

**Taxes**

Then there's taxes. As a general rule, anything that puts more money in people's pocket (lower taxes) stimulates consumer spending, creates jobs and is good for the economy. Anything that takes money out of people's pocket (higher taxes) creates less consumer spending, less jobs and is bad for the economy. This is perhaps the single most basic reality for the American economy yet our politicians cannot seem to grasp that simple and true concept. Our politicians spend money (YOUR money) like drunken sailors and then want MORE of your money to spend. The truth is that government spending is inefficient and wasteful. Consumer spending is efficient and productive ... and creates jobs which creates incomes which creates more spending which then creates more job, etc. And when more people have jobs, more people have incomes. And the more people there are who have incomes, and/or the higher the income, the more taxes the government gets. So, lower taxes creates more jobs and more income and more consumer spending and, as a result, the government collects MORE taxes.

Higher taxes creates few new jobs (and often causes a shrinkage of jobs), no new incomes, no new consumer spending and in fact, reduces all those good things. And, as a result of higher taxes, people get laid off or lose their jobs and that means fewer people are earning incomes and consumers will spend less ... and the government actually collects LESS tax money. So, that being the case, why would the government ever want to RAISE taxes??? Duh!

In a nutshell, that's how the basic American economy works.

**Drawbacks and advantages**

One of the fundamental things about capitalism is personal responsibility. Under capitalism you have to make it work for YOU. Under capitalism, if you and your family want to live well, or want the basics of food, shelter, clothing, personal transportation, a college education and medical care, you need money. And, if you don't inherit it, marry it, etc, to get money you have to work for it. You have to e-a-r-n it. That's your responsibility, as an individual. That's what makes capitalism difficult. But nobody said life was easy. Sure, who wouldn't want the basics of life to be provided, free of charge. Let someone else pay for it. Let the rich people pay for it. Let the government pay for it. Let it magically happen. In Ameri how adults think, that's how children think. As an adult, li work that way in America. For most Americans it's "You want i earn it". Many Americans say that's mean but, mean or not, that's still the way it is. And wishing and whining won't change it.

What the American economic system does allow is the opportunity to have a good life, to have a great life. To have the kind of life you want, with the freedom to live it the way you want to live it. Or get left behind and live in poverty. Is that fair? No. Is life fair? No. To succeed in life most of us in America have to:

1. get a good education
2. get a good job
3. work hard and long

And have some luck along the way.

And Wall Street is the epitome of capitalism. And opportunity. IF you have the aptitude and personality.

# Chapter 8 **Aptitude and Personality**

Wall Street demands that a worker have certain natural aptitudes and certain personality traits. Working on Wall Street is different than most normal jobs. It is not enough to be "normal" to work on Wall Street, you have to be "abnormal". "Normal" is defined as "what most people would do in a given situation". That being the case, as many people are seriously messed up … and often make bad choices … who wants to be normal?

What are the aptitudes and personality traits of Wall Streeters? Here is my unscientific selection of aptitudes and personality traits a Wall Streeter must, and should, have …

- College education, preferably majoring in finance, economics or business
- Very high aptitude for math
- Ability to work independently
- Ability to think independently

- Ability to create your own work
- Ability to work at fast pace
- Very high tolerance for risk
- Ability to live with extreme uncertainty
- Ability to handle extreme stress
- No fear of success. Or fear of money
- Un-afraid of taking chances
- Un-afraid to fail
- High level of confidence
- A healthy ego
- A driving desire to "win"
- A strong affinity for money
- Desiring a high standard of living
- High energy
- Financial creativity

A somewhat rare combination of aptitudes and traits? Yes. Wall Street is a numbers game not a people game. It's about the numbers and the math. And financially oriented information. And numbers and math and information are unemotional. Numbers and math are not compassionate or caring. Working on fast-paced Wall Street requires fast unemotional absorption of information and fast unemotional decision making. There is simply no time to ponder or dwell on the human side of the financial information gathered and used on Wall Street. That's one of the things that makes Wall Street so different. It's dispassionate. Like a good surgeon, who concentrates on the surgery and not on the emotional or financial well being of the patient he's cutting open.

To demonstrate what happens if you worked on Wall Street and did not have all the above traits here is a true story …
I was working in the municipal bond department of a prominent Wall Street investment banking firm. In the seat next to me was a very nice

gentleman named Bruce H. Over the months of sitting next to him I got to know him fairly well. Bruce was 37 years old . I was 23. Bruce told me that he had severe stomach ulcers - due to stress - which resulted in half of his stomach being removed. He was always stressed out and I saw that his job as a bond salesman was literally killing him. Finally, one day I asked him why didn't he quit and do something less stressful? He answered, "Because I have a wife, 2 daughters who will be going to college soon, a very large mortgage, and 2 car payments." I said, "It isn't worth it if you're dead." Then I asked Bruce what he would really like to do for a living instead of selling bonds. He said, "I always wanted to own a little hardware store. I would love to own a little hardware store in my town in New Jersey. I love hardware. I would sell nuts and bolts, no bonds." I urged him to do it, quit and open a hardware store in New Jersey, before he was dead, from stress, at the age of 40. Before he lost the other half of his stomach. Bruce thought about it for a minute. Then he went back to work. Selling bonds. A while later I happened to walk by his desk and noticed his W-2 form sitting there, face up. Bruce was away from his desk. Using one of the skills Wall Street people learn, the ability to read and absorb information very quickly, as I walked by I glanced down at this desk to see what he was working on, a normal Wall Street information function. I saw his W-2, his annual income. Then, I understood why Bruce was working selling bonds, and would continue to work selling bonds, even if it killed him. He did it for his family, for his wife and kids.

I saw his W-2, his annual income. In today's dollars, his annual income would be $1,200,000. One million two hundred thousand dollars.

Bruce, a genuinely nice guy and a fine human being, was working himself to death, for a million dollars a year. To provide for his family. Funny thing is, I don't think his family needed that level of income to be happy. And Bruce was not cut out to be a million-dollar-a-year bond salesman in New York on Wall Street. He was cut out to be a hardware store owner, in a small town in New Jersey.

Working yourself to death. For money. Is it worth it? Not to me. What good is it if you're dead? Yes, Bruce's wife and daughters would be well taken care of … but they wouldn't have Bruce, a wonderful husband and a wonderful father.

That was Bruce's choice. Life is series of choices. Choose wisely.

# Chapter 9 **Wall St - the Movie**

And then there's Gordon Gekko, the fictional superstar financial deal maker in the movie "Wall Street" (1987). The role of Gordon Gekko is a bit over-the-top, highly extreme, but basically accurate. And Gordon Gekko is a compelling character to watch in action. A review in the New York Times about Wall Street, the movie, tells us, "It's about Bud Fox (Charlie Sheen), a bright, blindingly ambitious young Wall Street broker who, on the strength of one insider tip, gains a spectacular career but loses his soul, at least temporarily. More important, it's also about Gordon Gekko (Michael Douglas), a corporate raider for whom ''rich'' isn't $450,000 a year, but rich enough to have your own jet."

''Wake up, pal,'' Gekko tells Fox. ''If you aren't inside, you're outside.'' Relying on information acquired by illegal hook and crook, Gekko buys up companies for peanuts and liquidates them for big bucks. ''I create nothing,'' he says with his usual candor. ''I own.''

Somewhere toward the middle of ''Wall Street,'' Gekko takes the microphone at the annual meeting of Teldar Paper, a company he's seeking to acquire, to deliver a pep talk on greed ...
''America has become a second-rate power,'' Gekko tells the Teldar shareholders. He cites the nation's horrendous trade imbalance and describes the backward state of domestic companies in competition with off-shore industry. Greed, he says, is all we have left, but greed is

also what made America great. It's normal. It's healthy and it's what keeps the system going. By the time Gekko finishes, the stockholders in tennis shoes are cheering.

According to film critic and reviewer, Roger Ebert, "Although Gekko's law-breaking would of course be opposed by most people on Wall Street, his larger value system would be applauded. The trick is to make his kind of money without breaking the law. Financiers who can do that, such as Donald Trump, are mentioned as possible presidential candidates, and in his autobiography Trump states, quite simply, that money no longer interests him very much. He is more motivated by the challenge of a deal and by the desire to win. His frankness is refreshing, but the key to reading that statement is to see that it considers only money, on the one hand, and winning, on the other. No mention is made about creating goods and services, to manufacturing things, to investing in a physical plant, to contributing to the infrastructure. What is missing is the "humanity".

What's intriguing about "Wall Street" - what may cause the most discussion … is that the movie's real target isn't Wall Street criminals who break the law. Director Oliver Stone's target is the value system that places profits and wealth and the Deal above any other consideration. His film is an attack on an atmosphere of financial competitiveness so ferocious that ethics are simply irrelevant …"

*Besides the fact that the real Wall Street DOES have ethics, it just has it's OWN set of ethics, the above reviews may be considered a fairly accurate depiction of the real Wall Street.*

# Chapter 10 **Big Egos/Big Salaries**

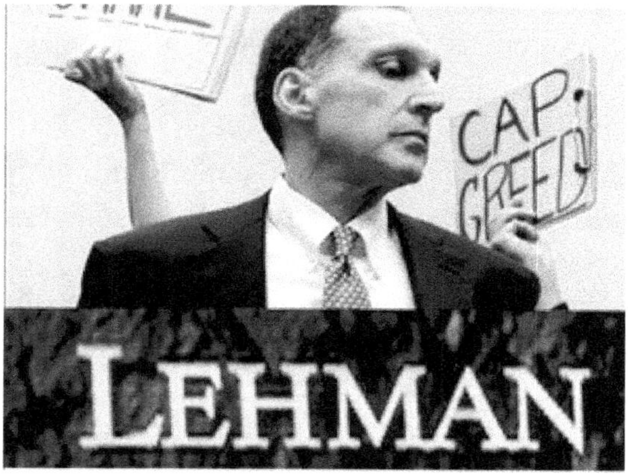


*Dick Fuld was Chairman and CEO of the now-defunct 150-year-old investment banking house of Lehman Brothers. He lives in a $32 million apartment on Park Avenue and is reported to be worth $500 million. Dick Fuld and the author started on Wall Street at the same place at the same time.*

According to the Office of State Controller, New York, "In 2010, the average salary in the securities industry in New York City … was … $361,330". Big salary? Yes.

However, the cost of living in New York City is also outrageously high.

Once upon a time, I lived in a very nice 2-bedroom apartment, in a doorman building, on the Upper East Side of Manhattan. My rent was $425 a month. I had 3 roommates. I was 23 years old. A few years later I moved around the corner to a loft apartment. With no roommates. Eventually, as rents went up, my loft apartment on the Upper East Side was $700 a month. A typical monthly parking space in the basement of a building close to my residence was $400 a month. In the summer months, using my 1 air conditioner, my electric bill was $200 a month.

Today, years later, indoor parking in my old neighborhood now costs about $600 a month. And today electric bills during the summer in Manhattan can run as high as $400 a month, for a tiny studio apartment, with 1 air conditioner.

Today a 2-bedroom apartment in the same building I once lived in currently rents for $4,180 a month, 10 times as much as when I lived there. And, according to CNN/Money, in 2011, "a two-bedroom apartment (to buy not rent) is listed for $1.43 million, about the average price in Manhattan". $1.4 million? Not a 6-bedroom house, an apartment! Two bedrooms? How many baths, one? And $1.4 million probably doesn't include any furniture. Or a parking space. Or utilities.

New York City is not a cheap city to live in. A decent salary in Manhattan today is probably $200,000. And, after taxes, that's barely breaking even.

Everything is expensive in New York. Plus, Wall Streeters have to dress well.

You don't go to work on Wall Street in jeans and a t-shirt. Or shorts. In New York, you wear a suit. Everywhere. Not a sports jacket, a suit. New York is a dressy place. And Wall Street demands a good fashionable professional image. You need 5-10 good fashionable suits, plus expensive accessories. Shirts, ties, coats, shoes and casual weekend wear. And an expensive watch. And maybe even expensive handmade shoes to go with your expensive suits. Handmade shoes? Yes, handmade shoes. Apparently, these days it's a Wall Street statement of style. And you need 4 complete sets of clothing, one for each season. It gets expensive. Very expensive.

Eating in a good restaurant in New York is not cheap either.

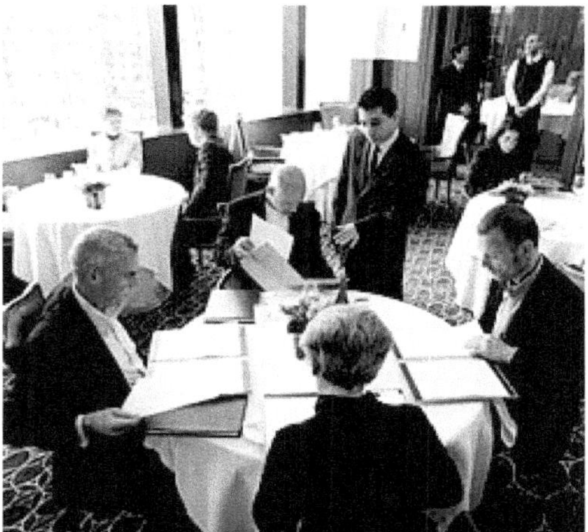

*Per Se restaurant, Manhattan*

A "good" restaurant in Manhattan today will probably cost you an average of $85-$100 for dinner for two people. And mixed drinks can cost up to $20, for one drink. Plus 9% tax and a 20% tip. The best restaurants costs more. The restaurant, "Per Se", at 60th and

Broadway, rated #1 by Zagat's restaurant guide, costs $295. Per person. Have I ever eaten there? No.
The cost of living in New York is high. Very high. Using CNN/ Money's cost of living calculator let's compare the cost of living in New York to the cost of living in Los Angeles in 2011. Compared to Los Angeles, things in New York will cost more. A lot more. In New York …

Housing will cost: 87% more
Groceries will cost: 45% more
Utilities will cost: 67% more
Transportation will cost: 6% more
Healthcare will cost: 19% more

So, if you make $100,000 a year in Los Angeles (and that's not a huge salary in L.A.) and think you are living well you'll need as much as $200,000 a year in New York in order to maintain the same lifestyle. $200,000. Before taxes. If you don't live extravagantly, you might be able to survive in Manhattan financially, on $200,000 a year. Barely. Maybe.

# Chapter 11 **High Results/High Pay**

How much pay is too much pay? If a superstar professional athlete earns $50 million a year no one says it's too much. If a music superstar earns tens of millions of dollars a year no one says it's too much. If a movie star gets $10 million or $20 million a picture no one says it's too much money. If ex-politician Al Gore earns a billion dollars promoting global warming no one says he earns too much. Why do these superstars earn so much money, tens, or hundreds, of millions of dollars a year? Because they make BILLIONS of dollars a year for their employer; the sports team owners, the record company, the movie studio, the nonprofit organization. Yet, when Wall Street superstars makes their employer hundreds of millions, or a billion dollars, in profits and they earn a couple of million dollars that year ... not as salary but as a BONUS ... everyone screams, "It's too much. They're greedy! They earn too much!" How much is too much? On Wall Street bonuses are calculated on a formula, based on performance. The bosses plug in the numbers and, if the formula says it's a bonus payout of a million dollars or 10 million dollars that's what it is. And, conversely, if the company makes NO profits that year the bonus may well be ZERO. Wall Streeters basically live on their salaries. A good salary. A high salary. The high salary pays for the high monthly cost of living in and around New York City, in a good neighborhood, with good schools, good restaurants and low crime. Wall Streeters live well. Because they have a good high-paying job. They have a good high-paying job because they have good, high-paying skills. They make the BIG money on bonuses. If there is a bonus that year.

By the way, for those of you who think Wall Street is too greedy and its workers make way too much money here is a little fact for you. The average annual salary of a stockbroker in 2010 was $67,470, according to CareerCast.com. That is less than the average schoolteacher's salary in California! According to California state figures, the average salary in 2010 for teachers in California was $67,932.

# Chapter 12 **Hedge Funds**

What are "hedge funds"? According to eHow.com, "Hedge funds are a type of diversified investment fund, similar to a mutual fund or an exchange-traded fund. Hedge funds are designed to help limit -- hedge against -- potential market risks. As an investor, it is important to know about some of the basic functions of hedge funds and the potential risks that come with them. Like most investment choices, the assets in a hedge fund may lose their value.

**Basics**

Hedge funds are a kind of collective investment. This means that they are composed of the pooled assets of multiple investors. As with stocks and mutual funds, this allows the managers of hedge funds to raise larger amounts of money by collecting investments in both small and large amounts. Hedge funds are also privately managed -- they are offered through an investment adviser rather than traded publicly on an open exchange.

**Functions**

Hedge funds are usually designed to manage risk and maximize gains through diversification. In contrast to stock investments, the money placed in a hedge fund is used to purchase various different kinds of financial instruments. They may purchase both the long and short sides of a transaction to hedge risk. Managers may use their fund's resources to invest in stocks, mutual funds, bonds and commodities, depending on their particular investment strategy. It's very important for those who invest in a hedge fund to know about how their money is to be used, and to talk with their financial adviser about the fund's strategy for financial growth.

**Types**

Hedge funds are usually classified according to their portfolio strategy. Different hedge funds carry different levels of risk according to the way they are managed. For example, aggressive growth hedge funds use their assets to buy stocks that are thought by fund managers to be poised for substantial growth in earnings per share. Income hedge funds, in another example, focus on investments like bonds with a more predictable yield.

**History**

While hedge funds have been used by investors in some form since 1949, they largely came to public popularity in 1966, after Fortune magazine profiled a major hedge fund that had significantly outperformed more traditional mutual funds. Between 1990 and the early 2000s, the assets held by hedge funds grew massively and began attracting investors from universities, charities and other major clients in addition to private individuals."

**Hedge fund pay**

Part of the mythology of modern Wall Street greed and outrageous pay stems from how much a hedge fund manager can make. It's often an outrageous amount of money, based on fees and bonuses. And results. The hedge fund managers are typically people you have never heard of. They are not famous nor do they normally seek the limelight. Possibly because they make so much money that they may be fearful of being exposed to the public, many of whom would likely be incredibly upset and angry at the disparity of income between what

a hedge fund manager earns in 1 year and what they, the average person earns ... in a lifetime.
How much did the top 10 hedge fund managers personally earn in 2010? Here is the list below. I did not divulge the hedge fund manager's name, for their own safety and security. The list is in reverse order, starting with #10.

#10. Earned $440 million
#9. Earned $450 million (#9 is a well-known extreme liberal socialist activist)
#8. Earned $640 million
#7. Earned $900 million
#6. Earned $1.1 billion
#5. Earned $1.3 billion
#4. Earned $2.2 billion
#3. Earned $2.5 billion
#2. Earned $3.1 billion

And, topping the list, The #1 highest paid hedge fund manager in 2010 personally earned a whopping $5.1 billion. That's 5.1 billion dollars. The #1 highest paid hedge fund manager earned over 5 billion dollars! In one year.

THAT'S real money! THAT'S Wall Street. THAT'S the real deal!

You want to know what the #1 highest paid hedge fund manager in 2010 looks like? Here is his photo ...

*He earned $5.1 billion. In 1 year*

# Chapter 13 **Why I Left Wall Street**

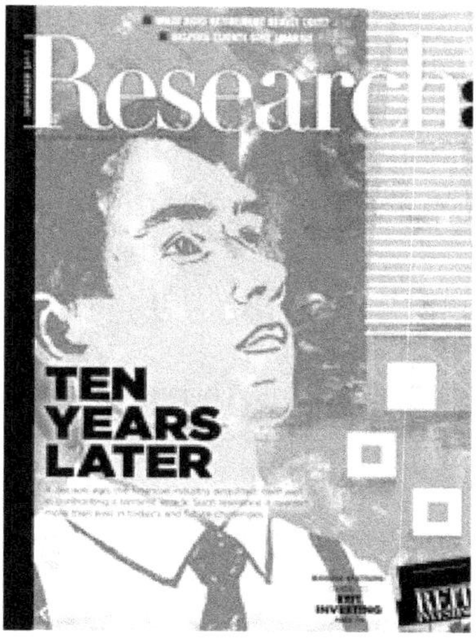


Ten years later I left Wall Street. Why? Because I was jealous that I didn't earn $5 billion? No, it wasn't because I didn't earn $5 billion. After a number of years I decided that Wall Street was simply no longer the right place for me. In the end all there was was the math. And the money. For me there was no feeling of ongoing accomplishment, no feeling of building something, anything. There was no "humanity", only endless numbers, numbers that fluctuated, all day every day. On Wall Street "you are only as good as your last trade". Too many years of too many extreme ups and extreme downs. One day you're a hero, making huge profits for your firm. The next day you're a dunce, losing huge sums of money for your firm. After a decade it took its toll on me. I wanted to be more "human", more normal, not a mathematical money making machine. Plus I was getting older. And my brain was getting tired.

Being on Wall Street, in the trenches, on the trading floor, is a young man's game. There is a saying on Wall Street. "There ARE no old traders".

So, what did I learn from working on Wall Street? A lot. Here is what

I learned …

I learned how to quickly and accurately absorb a lot of information and form an independent opinion. And then act on it.

I learned how to make huge important decisions, multi-million dollar decisions, in a split second. And live with the outcome.

I learned how to use my brain … until it hurt.

I learned the value of money. And the value of friendship and brotherhood.

I learned how to read upside down.

I learned, before computers, that when you made a verbal trade you honored it. Period. Your word was good. Your word was your bond.

I learned how to form, and value, my own opinion. On everything.

I learned how to keep my head while everyone around me was losing theirs.

I learned that I was not perfect.

I learned that sometimes you can be right and everyone else can be wrong.

I learned that sometimes everyone else can be right and you can be wrong.

I learned that often it is better to be lucky than smart. That sometimes it is better to be right for all the wrong reasons than to be wrong for all the right reasons.

I learned how to be, and act, like a professional.

I learned that I have limits.

I learned that I was not always as competent as I thought I was. And I learned to accept that and make it OK.

I learned why traders had an extra large bottle of aspirin and an extra large bottle of antacid tablets in their desk drawer.

I learned how to handle, and manage, enormous financial responsibility … and stress … at the tender age of 23.

I learned that I fit in almost everywhere. One night, at a party in my building, I taught the U.N. Ambassador from Panama how to use chopsticks. (I didn't know who he was until later).

I learned values and skills that have enriched my life beyond riches.

I learned how to think. Independently. To think for myself.

I learned that I looked really good in a suit.

In New York, in my early 20's, I learned how to be an adult. On Wall Street, in my early 20's, I learned how to be a man.

What did I learn on Wall Street? A lot. What I learned on Wall Street was … priceless.

In the end I left Wall Street. In search of humanity. More humanity. MY humanity. Many years later I realized that on Wall Street I really did help people, people all across America. I realized that I helped people all across America improve their lives. Because I realized that I was instrumental in helping hundreds of cities and states all across America to raise money … to build schools, hire teachers and police officers and fire fighters, build roads, bridges, airports, and even sports arenas … for the betterment of their community. I helped. From Wall Street. Doing my job. I helped make that possible. Indirectly, I helped millions of Americans have a better life. And I am proud of that.

# Chapter 14 **Wall Street Conspiracy Theories**

There are a number of conspiracy theories about money and Wall Street that I have heard over my entire lifetime. These conspiracy theories include:

**Jews own the banks and control all the money**

To the best of my considerable knowledge and experience no major commercial bank in the U.S. has ever been owned - or run - by Jews. In fact, it is extremely rare for a major U.S. commercial bank to even have a Jewish CEO. Historically and culturally, banks in the United States have always been owned, and run, not by Jews but by Wasps (White Anglo-Saxon Protestants). Historically and culturally, Jews do not usually go into commercial banking as a profession. Instead, Jews tend to enter the field of investment banking, which is totally different from commercial banking.

In the U.S. the banks, usually owned and run by white Anglo-Saxon Protestants (Wasps), are the real depositories of a lot of the money in the U.S. When the famous bank robber, Willy Sutton, was asked why he robbed banks he answered, "Because that's where the money is." The investment banks, often owned and run by Jews, do high-finance "deals" and figure out creative and highly profitable ways to USE the money that's in the banks. Banks are not owned by Jews; they're not even run by Jews. And Jews do not control all the money; nobody controls all the money.

**Rich people have all the money and they won't let us have any**

This is false. When it comes to money the rich are mainly concerned with their own wealth. Rich people do not prevent everyone else from having money. In America there's plenty of money to go around. You just have to get some for yourself. You have to put yourself in a situation where money flows to YOU. Money is not a zero sum game. It is not a closed circle. It is not true that if one person gets money someone else doesn't get any. That's not how money works. Money, like water, flows. Money can enter the U.S. system from other countries. Money can go from one sector to another. More money can be created; the U.S. Treasury can PRINT more money if more money is needed in the economy. There's plenty of money around and the rich just have more of it … but they don't have it all and they can't prevent YOU from getting it.

**You can't get rich in America anymore**

This is not true at all. America is still the land of opportunity and if someone (ANYONE) has a good idea, does all their research and business homework, learns what they need to know, applies themselves properly, and has the guts and perseverance to proceed, they can achieve the American dream. Yes, in America you can still invent something (you'll need to raise thousands of dollars for a patent) or start a business (from your kitchen table). To do that you have to get off your rear end and start turning your dream into a reality. Is it easy? No. Is it hard? Yes. Is it impossible? No, if you don't give up … and find a way! America loves new ideas and new products. It is the land of new ideas and new products and most new ideas, innovations and new products come from individuals and small businesses. Can you fail? Yes. Can you succeed? With hard work, desire, smarts, guts, and a little luck, yes. It is said that you learn nothing from success and everything from failure. The secret is to keep trying. Can you still get rich in America? Yes! For further inspiration just go online and, in your favorite search engine, enter "rags to riches stories".

**A small group of powerful people run the entire world**
Impossible. You can't get a group of people to agree on ANYTHING! Let alone how to rule the world. There are too many existing and competing local, regional, and national interests. However, the internet is a good example of a One World Philosophy, a world which has no borders, no time zones, no distances. If there was a small group of powerful people running the world they would certainly be owning and controlling the internet. Yet they don't. Hmm.

Most conspiracies about money, and Wall Street, simply are not true. Some conspiracies, on the other hand, might indeed be true. However, when it comes to conspiracy theories in general I say prove it, show me the f-a-c-t-s. Don't tell me your opinion, or someone else's opinion. Show me the f-a-c-t-s. Show me the facts that make s-e-n-s-e!

# Chapter 15 **Wall Street Stories**

Here are some personal stories from my Wall Street days, taken from my book, “Stories Of A Lifetime”. They are extraordinary stories. Of extraordinary events. They happened, they happened to me, and they are all 100% true …

**Real Money**

After I graduated from college and was deciding what to do with my life I made nightly visits to the local bars in my hometown in Upstate New York. One night I ran into a high school acquaintance, Donny W. I asked him what he’d been doing. He grinned and told me he had become a stockbroker at the local Bache & Co. Then he told me how much money he had already made in his first year. It was the equivalent of about $300,000 in today’s money. Wow, I thought. I knew I was smarter than he was and if he can make that much money I can certainly make that and more. This could be worth looking into! The next day I went downtown to Bache & Co and told them I was interested in becoming a stockbroker. The manager interviewed me, liked what he saw and told me I had to take a test before they would even consider hiring and training me. I said O.K. give me the test so you can hire and train me and I can make a lot of money. So I took the test. I got very high marks. The manager told me he had two other people already on the list to be hired before me and only had two openings so I would have to wait a while before he could hire me. That was a sign. And it started me thinking. If a person can make that much money playing around with stocks and math in a small town in Upstate New York, what could one expect in a big time place like New York City? Millions of dollars? So I set my sites higher. I would go to New York City, go see Merrill Lynch (the biggest stockbrokerage company), and become a stockbroker. Except that I had been to New York City maybe twice in my life, didn't know anybody at Merrill Lynch, and had nowhere to live there.

Then a little light bulb went off in my head. My parents had told me that a neighbor, Rick R., who was a few years older than I, lived in New York. I got his phone number from his parents and called him. He knew who I was. We talked for a bit and then he told me that his roommate had just left for Europe and he didn't know when or if the roommate was coming back so there was a roommate spot available right now if I wanted it.

Coincidence? I think not! I told my parents I was moving to New York City. They were shocked but understanding and encouraging. Two days later I boarded the NYC bound Greyhound bus with all my worldly possessions stuffed into two suitcases and one suit bag, with a grand total of $200 in my pocket.

The bus got into New York about 10PM. Suddenly, I realized that I didn't know my way around this gigantic place at all. How far away did this guy live? How much would it cost to get there? Luckily, he lived a short distance away in a good neighborhood on the East Side of Manhattan near the U.N. I arrived at my new residence and was greeted by Rick. He took me on a tour of the tiny one bedroom apartment. I was very tired from my trip and retired to my assigned bed. Tomorrow, bright and early, I was going down to Wall St. to Merrill Lynch headquarters to convince them to make me a stockbroker. I was 23 years old. I had no appointment.

Suddenly, at 2 o'clock in the morning, I realized that I didn't even know where Wall St. was! Or how to get there. Or where Merrill Lynch was located. Or who to see.

In the morning, before Rick went off to work, he told me how to get to Wall St. He told me about the subway. Subway? I had never taken a subway in my life! That morning, snappily dressed in my one and only suit, I took my first subway train ride. Ugh. The subway was noisy and crowded and filthy and scary. Thankfully, I took the correct train and did not end up fifty miles away. I exited the subway at the fabled Wall St stop.

Having realized that I didn't know anyone at Merrill Lynch and had no appointment to see anyone specific when I arrived which might just complicate my plan somewhat in becoming a stockbroker there, I had come up with a plan. I remembered a man who was sort of a family acquaintance and who worked on Wall Street at a major investment banking firm. It occurred to me that I should drop in on him and maybe he knew someone at Merrill Lynch and could introduce me or get me in to see the right person. Maybe he could help me become a Merrill Lynch stockbroker.

So, at 9:00 sharp I showed up unannounced at the prominent investment banking firm and asked the receptionist to inform Mr. Stone that I was there and could I have a minute of his time. I didn't know it at the time but normally Mr. Stone is never in the office, spending most of his time on the road, visiting clients of the firm. All over the world. Today, he was in. And I was invited in to see him.

We shook hands, he offered me a seat. Then he looked me over, evaluating me; I could see the wheels turning in his mind. I told him I wanted to be a stockbroker at Merrill Lynch and asked politely that if he knew anyone over there I would be appreciative. He responded to me that, first, he wanted to ask me a question. I told him to go ahead and ask. "What would you rather do," he posed, "try to get five thousand dollars out of Joe Blow from around the corner ... or try to get five million dollars out of a corporate treasurer?"

I paused and briefly considered the question.

Then I gave him my answer. "I like the sound of the 5 million", I said.

It must have been the right answer. Because he offered me a job. On the spot. I remember thinking that I had planned on being a stockbroker at Merrill Lynch but this was a golden opportunity and I'd be an idiot to pass it up.

I started that same day.

I got lucky. Very lucky. In a flash, I was now living in New York City and had a job on Wall Street with a 150-year-old prestigious investment banking house.

I never did make it to Merrill Lynch. I never did become a stockbroker. Do I regret not becoming a stockbroker? Never.

**First Week On Wall St**

I was not in stocks. I was in the short term money markets. Where large financial and corporate institutions borrowed money or invested their money for short periods of time. The minimum investment was $5 million. A typical workday for trainees was from 7AM to 7PM. The markets were open for actual trading from 9AM to 2:30PM but there was a lot of daily preparation and follow-up that was necessary. Each morning I read three newspapers; The New York Times, The Wall St. Journal and The New York Post ... all before 7AM. On Sunday, I read the entire Sunday New York Times. Being prepared, keeping abreast of not only the financial news but current events and general news as well was critical to the job; we had to know about anything that could impact the markets. Before anyone else. Our investment clients relied on us to provide them information, direction and understanding of the nuances of interest rate movements, on a minute-to-minute basis.

I immersed myself in the job. I was a general all around gofer, very busy trying to absorb all the fundamentals of the markets. Very busy just trying to keep up. This was on-the-job training. This was training under fire.

I had taken several finance and economic courses in college and, occasionally would ask one of the professional traders or sales people a question about why things were not done according to what I had been taught in school. Sometimes they smiled tolerantly, sometimes they chuckled, and sometimes they rolled on the floor laughing. They explained that if it was done like what they taught in school it simply wouldn't get done. Not enough time. In the real world, on Wall Street, things had to be done lightning quick thus many shortcuts had to be established to accommodate the reality of doing trillions of dollars of business ... every day.

Quickly, I unlearned everything I had been taught in school and started learning the practical real world techniques of professional

Wall St. investing.

The pressure was intense. Everyone had phones on their desk. When the phones weren't ringing the traders and sales people were often talking on two or more phones at the same time. Lots of action. Fast action. Non-stop fast action. One day towards the end of my first week the head trader thought I was too hesitant and too slow doing one of the tasks assigned to me. I was about ten feet away from him. He screamed at me. Then he picked up one of the phone systems on his desk and threw it at my head! Luckily, he missed.

Somehow, I survived my first week.

**The Eight-Million-Dollar Mistake**

After only two weeks on the job I received a promotion.

They put me in charge of a whole department. A one-person department. Me; I was the department. I was now in charge of raising money for an agency of the United States government; the Federal National Mortgage Association (Fannie Mae) in Washington, D.C.

How it worked was that there were four major dealers who were authorized to issue short term Fannie May discount notes. Each dealer was paid a commission for this by Fannie Mae. Each day we were given an allotment, a maximum amount of money to raise for Fannie Mae that day. This helped Fannie Mae budget and smooth out the cash flow they needed to support the mortgage financing markets. Usually, they wanted to raise a few million dollars. Sometimes Fannie Mae didn't need any money at all on a given day. Management of this capital raising function rotated each week between the four dealers. Brand new to all this, my mentor, Paul, who was assigned to train me, briefly showed me how to do everything. Then, it was our turn to become the manager, run the book, manage the sales, report to Fannie Mae, etc.

I was on my own, running a whole department! The other dealers would call me up and request an amount of money against orders they had generated. I filled all their orders and kept track of the sales. At the end of the day I would notify the director of our firm and then Fannie Mae about how much we had raised for them that day. That day I had raised 12 million dollars and was very proud. I told Paul how much business I and the other dealers did. His jaw dropped. "Twelve million?" he gasped. "That sounds like an awful lot. How much was the allotment today?" I gave him a blank look. He ran over to my Fannie Mae book and looked down at the official allotment I had received and written in for that day. Four million. Paul turned ghostly white. "Oh, lord", he wailed, "we are in deep doo-doo. You were only allowed to raise four million dollars today and you raised twelve!" He immediately ran in to see the boss. A director of the firm. I could see them through the glass walls of the boss's office; we called it the fishbowl. Paul spoke briefly to him. Then the director's face turned red. Very red. Then he started to scream at Paul. Then he stuck his head out of the door of the fishbowl and screamed for me to get in there. NOW! I entered the fishbowl with my knees shaking. At the top of his lungs the director screamed and screamed at me. "You stupid son-of-a-bitch! You raised eight million dollars more than you were allowed! Now I have to call the president of goddamn Fannie Mae in goddamn Washington, D.C. and see if I can figure out a way to correct this friggin mess! If I goddamn can't, we'll have to cough up the extra eight goddamn million dollars out of our own goddamn pockets!!!"

Oh goddamn, I thought, I'm dead. My life is over.

The director told me to wait outside. Then he called Washington and spoke to the president of Fannie Mae. He explained about the "new kid" and the mistake. They worked out a deal; Fannie Mae honored the extra eight million dollars of notes sold by me even though they didn't need the money right then and it could be a bit of political problem et al. And seeing as how I made them "overspend" their budget by eight million dollars that day they probably wouldn't need anymore money raised by us, by me, for a while, thank you very much.

I was saved! Or so I thought. The director screamed at me some more. Then he screamed at Paul again. Then he screamed at me again. Then he finally calmed down a little.
He looked at me, hard, and told me he was now going to tell me something I would never forget. And he said,

"He who sells what isn't his'n - delivers same - or goes to prison"

Gulp. I went pale (or even paler if that was possible under the circumstances).

I heard that little saying only one time. And for the rest of my life I never forgot it.

It took me a long time to get over making that eight-million-dollar mistake.

Somehow, I survived it.

And, to this day, I have never feared making a mistake again. Any mistake.

After all, once you make an eight-million-dollar mistake it isn't very likely that you could ever make a mistake that big again!

**Toys**

I was now 23 years old. And a money market professional on Wall St. I began making money. I began spending money. I didn't know what to buy first. So, I bought a few nicer, more expensive suits and assorted clothing for the different seasons (in New York, you end up with a summer wardrobe, a fall wardrobe, a winter wardrobe and a spring wardrobe; it raises hell with your closet space but four wardrobes are a definite necessity). Then, I bought some toys. I bought a new Sony Trinitron 17" TV (it just came out that year and was quite a revolutionary TV at the time) for the equivalent of $1,500 in today's money. I purchased a JVC videotape machine (the first model for consumer/home use) for $790, which in today's money would be about $2,500-$3,000. I bought cameras and camera equipment and all sorts of toys, both expensive and inexpensive.

Then, about three months later, I looked around my cluttered 2-bedroom New York City apartment and realized I had no room left. I thought maybe this is a good time to stop the spending spree. I basically now had all the toys I really wanted anyway. And I had no real interest in buying super big ticket items like a house, or a car (useless and a liability in Manhattan) or a boat. Or an airplane. Or spending money just for the sake of spending.

So I made a deal with myself. The deal was that I allowed myself to spend up to $100 on any item I wanted; anytime, anywhere. On impulse. No sense being deprived if you're 23 and have serious money coming in! However, if an item cost more than $100, I could not buy it on impulse; I had to first decide if I really, truly, honestly wanted it. If the honest answer was yes, I was allowed to buy it. If the true and honest answer was no, I had to refrain from purchasing it. How did I do that? I asked the little voice in my head.

With great discipline, I honored the little voice in my head and the deal with myself.

And, as a result, shortly thereafter I found that I really, truly, honestly wanted a lot less stuff than I thought. I stopped spending lavishly. I discovered that when I had enough money to buy or do anything I wanted, eventually the thrill of spending and accumulating stuff simply wears off. Eventually. I didn't become a miser or a cheapskate or put myself on a strict budget but I did begin buying only the things I needed or things that would last that I really wanted to own.

At age 23, I had learned another valuable lesson about money. And, by not spending it all, I began to accumulate some. Older people called it savings!

## The Five-Billion-Dollar Heist

I used to take one of my Wall Street clients, Ed, to lunch. Ed was the short-term investment manager for five New York City pension funds. The five New York City pension funds, at that time, had investments of over 5 billion dollars.

We went to lunch often. We always ate excellent and expensive lunches. I always paid.

One day, Ed told me a secret. He told me that the City of New York physically stored the short-term investments for the five pension funds they managed in a vault. The vault was down the hall from his office. He told me the investments were mainly in 100% negotiable U.S. Treasury bills. And that there were approximately five billion dollars worth of negotiable U.S. Treasury bills just sitting there in the vault. I was suitably impressed. Then he told me that the officials of the city didn't know how much was in there. Nobody paid attention. Nobody ever took an inventory. Ed told me that, as an investment person, he had unlimited access to the vault. He told me that if he wanted he could just walk right into the vault. He could just walk right into the vault, carrying his briefcase. He could just walk right into the vault carrying his briefcase, and in five minutes he could pack up five billion dollars worth of negotiable U.S. Treasury bills, and walk right out.

He said it would be years before the City even knew it was gone!

We pondered that for a few minutes. Simple. Easy. Just the two of us in on it. It really would work! Five billion dollars of Treasury bills. Easily converted into cash. But that much probably had to be fenced through the mob (assuming there was a mob) and we'd be lucky to clear two billion in cash. Split two ways was a billion each. Cash. My God, I thought. With a billion dollars in cash I could skip the country, buy a tropical island, complete with voluptuous native girls, be the king of my own tropical island, and, as king and absolute ruler, declare a no-extradition policy with the United States!

Ed and I just looked at each other. Figuring it out.

After a few moments of very serious pondering, both of us, at the same time, smiled and said, “Nah, it’s not us. It’s not who we are.”

We finished our excellent and expensive lunches, left the restaurant and went back to our jobs.

I believe that that day we were both given a test. A test of temptation. A monumental test of temptation. A supreme test of moral fiber and character. We both passed the test. For isn’t it a supreme test, a sign of good character ... if you are presented with an absolutely real and easy opportunity to steal five billion dollars ... and don’t?

**Oh, Mr President**

One day on Wall Street, as I was sitting next to one of the other traders, the most absolutely amazing thing happened. This story is absolutely, 100% as-God-is-my-witness true ...

It was the day of the start of the NBA Professional Basketball Championship Finals, between the NY Knicks and the Los Angeles Lakers. Tip-off was scheduled for 8:00PM. The game was to be carried live on TV. The trader next to me, Roy S., was an avid Knicks fan. I mean rabid, fanatic. I'm sitting there doing my work when all of a sudden Roy starts cursing. Not unusual in a trading room but this seemed personal. I look over and ask him what's the matter. He points to the electronic Dow Jones newswire that ran across the front of our trading room. Across the Dow Jones wire comes the message that the President of the United States will be giving a speech tonight - live - at 8 o'clock. Roy is livid. He starts screaming that the president's speech will interfere with the broadcast of the NBA Playoff Game. I tell him that's too bad but it's the President of the United States -- what can you do?

Roy continues to steam.

I go back to work. A minute or two later, I hear Roy dialing Information for Washington, D.C. and then ask for the phone number of the White House. I look over smiling, thinking it's a joke.

Then I see Roy dial the number and then he asked, "Is this the White House?"

Now, I am utterly shocked; this is no longer a joke. This could be big trouble.

Roy is now giving his real name and real phone number and real address to the White House operator. "Oh, Christ," I mutter to myself, "now we're dead." Any second I expect the Secret Service to come busting into the trading room, guns drawn, and arrest us all.

What in hell is Roy doing???

Now, mouth agape, I lean closer to hear everything he is saying.

Roy tells the White House Operator that the President probably doesn't realize that his speech will be interfering with the start of the basketball finals game tonight and could the president reschedule his speech at another time or maybe wait until after the NBA finals are over.

The White House operator apparently gave him an unsatisfactory response.

Roy then says, "Well, then who's in charge of scheduling the president's speeches?" The operator responds. Roy says, "OK, then connect me with the Press Secretary."

I am flabbergasted. I can't believe this!

Roy continues, "Hello. Is this the Press Secretary? Good. Would you please tell the President that his speech tonight will be interfering with the first game of the NBA Playoff Finals and that he needs to reschedule the speech."

Where are those Secret Service agents? They should have been here by now.

Roy says thank you very much and hangs up the phone. Then he calmly goes back to work.

I'm looking at him like he's an alien from another planet (which after what he just did maybe he IS an alien from another planet).

Not five minutes later, scrolling across the Dow Jones newswire, for the whole world to see, came the following message ...

**The NBA Playoff Game Tonight Will Be Shown In It's Entirety Directly After The President's Speech**

# Chapter 16 **Greed, Corruption and Stupidity**

The Great Mortgage Meltdown of 2008 and the resulting catastrophic financial crisis on Wall Street, Main St, in the banking industry and in the government? Who was at fault? Who was to blame? Everybody! It was a monumental case of greed, corruption and stupidity. It was a "perfect storm". Let's take a quick look at everyone's role - and everyone's failure - that caused this worldwide Depression-like financial crisis ...

**The government**

The idea. Starting with Bill Clinton, and promoted and protected by U.S. Congressman Barney Frank, of Massachusetts, the federal government decided it was a great idea if more Americans owned a home. If EVERYONE in America who wanted a home could get one. Unfortunately, to buy a home in America and get a mortgage you needed a substantial down payment and enough income to pay the mortgage. Not a problem, said the government. Let's make it so a person didn't need to qualify properly, didn't need a big down payment OR an income. Let's get our Federal National Mortgage Association to lower the standards, or do away with the tough standards altogether, and then we'll force the banks who issue the mortgages to give a mortgage to practically anybody, even people who do not qualify for a mortgage. Risky? Sure. But we don't care, we're the government and it's a great idea politically. We, the federal government, will just sort of "quasi guarantee" the risk. So they did. And, because of the pressure from Washington, and the "elimination" of risk, banks happily issued billions and billions of dollars of mortgages … to people who would never normally qualify … to people who did not have enough income to pay the mortgage if the floating interest rate on their mortgage went up … or to people who had no income at all (they lied on the mortgage application and it was not verified or checked). And, so it was. Thanks to the government, the American Dream of home ownership became a reality. For everyone. For anyone. Regardless of employment or income. Or the ability to pay the mortgage (if the floating rate went up). And, for years, everyone was happy. Especially all those people who now owned a home who could never afford to own a home. What a great concept! Until the sh-t hit the fan … and millions of those low/no income homeowners couldn't pay back the loan, couldn't pay the mortgage, because the low low rate they originally got was a floating rate, and it floated up. Way up. Suddenly the dream became a nightmare. And the nightmare became the Great Mortgage Meltdown, which threatened to crash the entire world economy. It could never have happened without the U.S. government wanting to make home ownership affordable for every American, whether they could afford it or not. It was a stupid idea gone bad. And a bad idea gone stupid.

**Wall Street**

What Wall St did, to take advantage of a potentially huge and profitable market, was put a bunch of mortgages and other things together in a "package" and created a type of security which they could then sell. The problem was that some of the stuff, about 10%, in the "package" was potentially "bad" or risky mortgages, which could default, become worthless, and mess up the value of everything else in the package. A good analogy is a barrel of apples. Let's say you have a barrel of 100 apples. You can't see every apple but you are assured - more or less guaranteed - that they will all be good, and told maybe only 5 apples might become rotten, leaving 95 edible apples. And the federal government will make good on the 5 bad apples. Thus, the barrel looks like a pretty good investment. And the barrel is even rated AAA by the official apple barrel rating agencies. AND has an implied guarantee from the U.S, government. Billions of dollars of these apple barrel securities were sold. As an investment. As an investor (bank, insurance company, etc) it looked like a good solid investment. It wasn't. It was garbage cleverly disguised and packaged as something edible. Yes, 90% of the security was fine, 10% of what was inside the package was potentially toxic. When 10% of the apples (mortgages) in the barrel went bad, no one could figure out what the whole barrel was then worth. And if a security and the market for that security is deemed untradeable, because no one could figure out what that security is worth, the accounting rules say you have to make it worth $0 … and take it as a total loss. It's called "mark to market". It's the "mark to market" rule that caused the real problem. And all that was needed to avoid the financial Mortgage Meltdown was to simply suspend the "mark to market" rule. The U.S. federal government, in particular the Treasury Secretary of The United States, refused to do that. And that triggered the massive catastrophic worldwide financial market meltdown.

In my experience and opinion these "apple barrel" mortgage backed securities should never have been created by Wall Street. In the "old days" of Wall Street, when you went to your boss with an idea for creating a new investment security they listened … and then told you why it would not work. Because the bosses had integrity, a clear sense of right and wrong, and decades of hands-on knowledge and experience. They knew what garbage was and would never allow it to be created and/ or pollute the markets. These mortgage based security packages should NEVER have been created, let alone sold. Stupid, stupid, stupid! Why? Because they contained obvious potentially rotten apples … lousy risky mortgages. Lousy risky mortgages given to low/no income homeowners who, if interest rates rose on their floating rate mortgage, could not possibly pay their mortgage over 10, 20 or 30 years. That is exactly what happened. Millions of homeowners defaulted. They stopped paying their mortgage. Their "rotten apple mortgage" was part of the "apple barrel" that was packaged and sold, by the billions, as a good solid investment. When those rotten apple mortgages defaulted, went rotten, the entire barrel became suspect ... and potentially worthless. And suddenly the federal government's "implied" or "quasi" guarantee evaporated into thin air. And thus was caused the largest worldwide financial panic since the Great Depression of 1929.

**Ratings Agencies**

In the old days the major Wall Street bond rating agencies, Moody's, Standard and Poors, and Fitch, were 100% accurate, 100% reliable, 100% dependable - and 100% incorruptible - as to rating the risk of an investment security. They were very strict in their rating criteria. They could be depended upon to issue proper and conservative bond ratings which could be used as proper and conservative guidelines for major institutional investors in bonds, investors such as banks, insurance companies, governments, pension funds and mutual funds. It should have been obvious, to anyone in the bond rating business with more than 1 year of experience, that the low/no income mortgages packaged together with good mortgages and other good securities, was a poor and very risky investment. Rotten apples. Yet the rating agencies gave these rotten apple mortgage investments their highest rating. Why? Stupidity? Corruption? Greed? All of the above?

**Who's blameless?**

The investors are blameless. Banks, insurance companies, mutual funds and other institutional investors who invested in rotten apple barrel mortgage securities did so based on the AAA rating by the bond rating agencies. That is the golden standard of investing. These investors followed 100% proper investment protocol. And got screwed.

The low/no income homeowner is blameless; if a bank or mortgage broker offers you a home you can't possibly afford and shows you that you CAN afford it, what do you do? You buy the home. Was it too good to be true? Yes, but all the "authorities" lined up and made it possible. At least for a while.

The Federal Reserve is blameless. The rotten apple mortgage securities were, like many securities, simply not on the list of securities that the Fed closely monitored.

The mortgage meltdown was a perfect storm. Everybody goofed. Everybody got greedy. Everyone got stupid. The government, Wall Street, the bond rating agencies, the banks, the homeowners. All of them were stupid. Or greedy. Or stupid AND greedy. All fell in line, together. All the elements came together - to form what would become the perfect storm. And create the largest worldwide financial panic and meltdown since the Great Depression of 1929. Could it have been avoided? Yes. Should it have been avoided? Yes. But things do happen. As they say, "sh-t happens". Rarely, things come together and form a catastrophic perfect financial storm. And that is what happened in the Mortgage Meltdown of 2008. Could it happen again? Yes. But it will probably be something else, a financial catastrophe in another form. Why can it happen again? It is the nature of things.

# Chapter 17 **Investing**

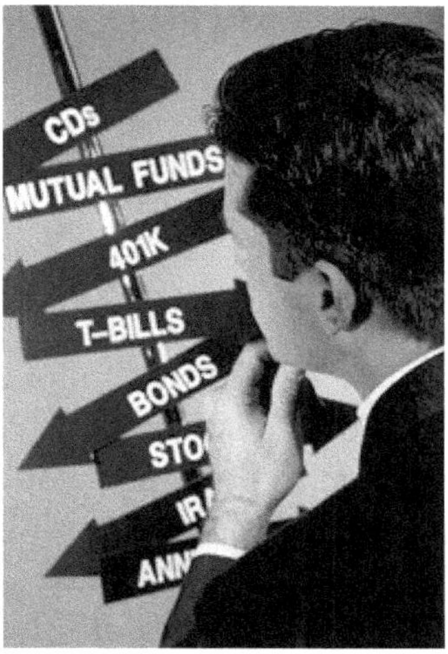


So, you want me to tell you the secret of successful investing? OK, I will. Here is the secret of successful investing. Don't invest. Don't do it. Only kidding! Before we talk about investing I want to point out an important point about investing. As I am not currently licensed to give investment advice I can't give you any specific information regarding investments. I can, however, give you some wisdom. First, you have to HAVE some money in order to invest it. You don't need a lot of money to start investing but you do need some. And once you have some money to invest you don't want to lose it.

Let me say that again. Once you accumulate money try not to lose it. That's the #1 rule of wealthy people (and the #1 fear of wealthy people).

You don't want to lose your money. You don't want to lose your money by squandering it, being the victim of a scam, or by making bad investments.

**Squandering money**

If you suddenly find yourself with a lot of extra money … or more money than you ever dreamed of having … STOP! Before you go on any huge and expensive spending sprees stop, sit down, take a deep breath, and relax. Once you get past the shock that you no longer have to worry about money you'll want to be careful not to lose, or spend, it all.

Here's how to do that …

1. Determine how much extra money you actually have. Is it taxable? If so, after taxes, you'll end up with less money to spend. So figure out how much you'll have after taxes.
If you have an extra million dollars, and don't invest it, and spend $50K a year it will only last you 20 years. If you invest a million dollars at 5% it will earn you $50,000 a year
… and you'll always have the original million dollars.

2. Decide what you want to do with your money. Do you want to pay off your debts? Take a long deserved vacation? Buy a new house or car? Save it for your kids college education? Give it away? Or pretend you don't have it and put it in the bank. Or put it under your mattress (not recommended).

3. If you're not an experienced money manager see a professional immediately, before you make a mess that you might regret. Find a reputable CPA or financial counselor who
specializes in financial planning and go see them. Discuss your financial needs and desires with the financial professional and he or she will design a financial plan that fits you.

**Beware of scams**

There's no shortage of scams which try to separate you from your money. Long lost relatives (who may not be your relatives at all), bogus business and investment deals, pie-in-the-sky ridiculously high potential rates of returns, all manner of internet schemes, telephone and mail solicitations that want you to divulge your banking info, the list goes on and on.

How do you know if something is a scam? Personally, I am always a bit skeptical about ANY potential investment and assume any investment may be not as good as advertised, may be a bad investment or may be a scam or something that may result in a loss of my money. And, of course, **if something sounds too good to be true, it probably is.** Be wary and trust your instincts. And be prepared to walk away … fast.

OK, now here are the real secrets to successful investing …

**Making investments**

No matter what the economic conditions are there's no shortage of investments that can turn out bad. Remember the dot.com bubble? The housing bubble? The mortgage meltdown?

In the 1990's many people put a lot of their money into the stocks of brand new, untried high tech companies and saw a huge run up in stock profits. This was followed by a huge crash of these same stocks, which wiped out investors' profits AND their original investment. There were individuals who blindly invested their savings, their kids college fund, borrowed against their home to invest more money and thought their dot.com stocks would keep going up forever. They were wrong. The dot.com bubble eventually burst and they lost all their money.

A similar thing happened with real estate in America from the late 1990's to 2007. Real estate values kept going up and up and up. That bubble burst and a lot of people found their real estate investments went way down in value. And millions of homeowners lost their homes. And their investment.

<u>Every hot investment eventually cools off. Every investment bubble eventually bursts.</u>

**The secret of investing**

The secret of investing is to know when to get in and when to get out. Simple … but not easy. Here's a true story to demonstrate this secret …

I was working on Wall St when the U.S. went off the gold standard in 1971. Gold was selling for $35 an ounce. Suddenly, gold prices started going up. I watched the price of gold go up. And up. And up some more. When it approached $300 an ounce, based on the research I had done I decided it was a good investment and, though it had already gone up from $35 an ounce to $300 an ounce, I thought it had the potential to go to $500 an ounce or more. I had a bunch of extra money and decided to invest it in gold, knowing that I could replace the money if I lost it. So, being financial able to take some risk, I bought gold at $300 an ounce. The price of gold went up. And up. And up. $350. $400. $450. $500. When it hit $600 an ounce. I was tempted to sell. If I sold I would have doubled my money. Not bad. But what if gold went even higher? I would make even more money. Greed. On the other hand, what if it went down and I ended up breaking even or losing my money? Fear. I didn't know what to do. So I looked at the available research again, and, as the price of gold continued to go up, I decided to stay in at $600 an ounce. It kept going up. $650 an ounce. $700 an ounce. $750 an ounce! Now, I had to consider selling and taking a HUGE profit. But when should I sell? Gold was still going up. Should I stay in and hope it kept going up or take my profit now, even though gold could go substantially higher. Or the market could crash. Greed versus fear. While I was wrestling with the "sell/don't sell" issue, one evening I happened to take a taxi home from Wall St. The taxi driver started telling me about gold; he told me he had been watching the news (which for some time had been reporting on the meteoric rise in the price of gold). The cabbie was very excited about investing in gold. He thought that the price of gold would go up even further, and keep going up. He was getting ready to invest his hard earned money in gold! I listened intently. This went on for 15 minutes. Then I told him to forget about dropping me off at my home and that instead he should take me straight to a different address, which I gave him. It was the address of my gold dealer. I arrived at the gold dealer's place of business, walked in, and cashed in my entire gold investment.

At $790 an ounce. The next day the price of gold hit $800 (for about a minute) and started dropping. It dropped like a stone. And kept dropping. The gold bubble had burst. Eventually, the price of gold dropped all the way back from $800 to $300 an ounce, wiping out everyone who bought gold at over $300 an ounce and stayed in it. I sold it at the top. How did I know when to buy and when to sell a hot investment? First, before I jumped in, I watched it for awhile. I waited for the price to start going up, I waited for it to start getting hot. I researched it before I bought in; I read everything I could find about the investment outlook. Then I invested. How did I know when to sell? The taxi driver. When the "public" (the average person) gets excited about getting into an investment (stocks, real estate, commodities, etc,) jumps on the bandwagon and starts investing in a market that's been red hot for quite a while that's when the professionals start getting out. That's the top. That's how I knew when to sell. No, I am not being elitist. The truth is that, by the time the media and the public take notice of a hot investment, and consumers keep hearing about it, that investment has already been hot for quite a while. That's what makes it newsworthy to the public. And that's when the professionals sell and get out. And leave the "last guys to get in" holding the bag. The moral of the story is: **don't invest like an amateur, invest like a professional.** How do professionals invest? They do their homework. They study investment information. They read the Wall St journal and other financial and investment publications. Every day. They educate themselves about investing. They l-e-a-r-n. And, hopefully, they make more good investment than bad investments. Do investment professionals make bad investments. Yes. However, to put it into prospective, a major league baseball player who consistently hits .300

or better is considered a star. And he's only successfully hitting the ball 3 times out of 10!

In the U.S., markets are usually controlled by professionals inside the markets. Traders and professional institutional investors are normally the ones that move a market up or down. No, I am NOT saying it's a conspiracy, I am saying that's how markets work. From the "insiders" to the "outsiders". From the professionals to the amateurs. If you are not an "insider" (defined as a professional who actually works daily in an investment area) then you are an outsider. The professional has the advantages of being in the middle of the action, right there, getting market and research information quickly and being able to buy and sell instantly.

When it comes to investing, do your homework like a professional, think like a professional, invest like a professional, and take profits like a professional. What's the secret of how professionals make profits? They buy low … and sell high.

**Investing wisely**

There is an old Wall St acronym about investing money. The acronym is S.L.Y. SLY stands for Safety, Liquidity and Yield.

**Safety**

Safety first. Safety means investing with low or no risk. Low or no risk investments include Treasury bills, U.S. government bonds, municipal bonds, bank CD's (insured by the FDIC), long term mutual funds, etc.

**Liquidity**

Liquidity means that an investment can be easily and readily converted into cash. Usually in a matter of days (or less). Liquid investments include stocks, bonds, mutual funds and other stock market related investments, insurance policies, gold, diamonds, etc. Liquidity is important because you don't want all your money tied up in things you can't readily convert into cash. Why? Because you might suddenly need a substantial amount of ready cash. For a better investment opportunity, for purchasing a new or additional home, for buying a private airplane or a boat, or for a catastrophic illness in the family that is not fully covered by your health insurance. Or because the value for that investment is about to go down, permanently

**Yield**

Last comes yield. Yield means the rate of return on your investment. The higher the rate of return the higher the risk. Sure, everyone wants to earn 25% … 50% … 100% a year on their investments but high returns often means high risks, and high risk means you could lose your money. And rule #1 is: once you have money try not to lose it. If you do have extra money, extra money you can afford to lose (and are willing to lose), and you have the personality for it, then some speculation or high risk investing can be exciting, fun, potentially very profitable, and can add extra zing to your love life!

If you are going to invest, invest wisely.

# Chapter 18 **Funny Money**

And, for a bit of fun, on the subject of money and wealth and Wall Street here are some of the author's favorite quotes …

"Money can't buy you happiness but happiness can't buy you money."
- *Andrew Lawrence*

"Those who say that money can't buy happiness probably have no money."
- *Andrew Lawrence*

"Those who say that money can't buy happiness are shopping in the wrong stores."
- *Andrew Lawrence*

"There are more important things in life than money. Try and name 10."
- *Andrew Lawrence*

“There’s no such thing as being too healthy or too wealthy.”
*- Andrew Lawrence*

“It is better to be filthy rich than filthy poor.”
*- Andrew Lawrence*

“The rich are different. They have more money”
*- Ernest Hemingway*

“There is only one group of people in society who thinks more about money than the rich, and that’s the poor.”
*- Oscar Wilde*

“Money doesn’t make you happy. I now have $50 million, but I was just as happy when I had $48 million.”
*- Arnold Schwarzenegger*

“I’ve got all the money I’ll ever need, if I die by four o’clock.”
*- Henny Youngman, comedian*

# Chapter 19 **What's Right/Wrong with America**

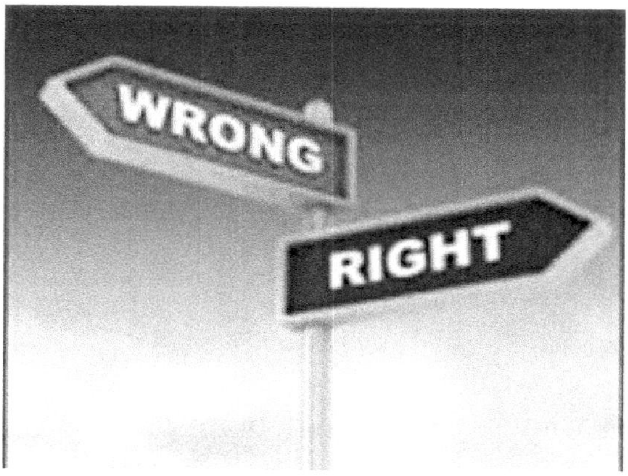


Published: Tuesday, June 14, 2011
By Greg Awtry, Publisher
York News-Times

What's right with America?

Democracy — actually we are a republic, but we do hold democratic elections to elect people to represent us.

What's wrong with America?

Only about half of all Americans care enough about our country to vote.

What's right with America?

Our Military — America's military defends our land, our freedoms and our national interests without question.

What's wrong with America?

Politicians and presidents who send our troops to foreign lands claiming it is in our national interest, when clearly it is not. (Iraq and Libya for example)
What's right with America?

Compassion —America races to disasters around the globe, using our great wealth and human resources to help people in need.

What's wrong with America?

We give America's wealth away by the billions in the name of foreign aid to countries who may not need it, or misuse it.

What's right with America?

We have led the world in innovation by leading the world in education.

What's wrong with America?

We have lost our lead in innovation and education.

What's right with America?

Religion — We were smart to separate religion and government.

What's wrong with America?

We are losing our Christian values.

What's right with America?

Manufacturing — We take America's vast natural resources and high quality workers to produce products with the "Made in the United States" label, the best in the world.

What's wrong with America?

What's still made in America?
What's right with America?

Health care — We have the finest health care in the world.

What's wrong with America?

Obamacare, ordering free American citizens to buy health insurance or be fined by the Internal Revenue Service.

What's right with America?

Laws — We are a land of laws intended to protect and preserve our nation and our citizens.

What's wrong with America?

A Federal government that won't enforce its own laws.

What's right with America?

Social Security and Medicare, two programs designed to take care of our nation's senior citizens.
What's wrong with America?

Politicians who are afraid to fix the broken systems because it may cost them votes.

What's right with America?

States' rights — Fifty states have united to create a magnificent nation, yet maintain their own individual constitutions.

What's wrong with America?

A Federal government that either is set on trampling states rights or blackmailing states to giving up those rights by withholding federal dollars.

What's right with America?

Sovereignty — We Americans are a sovereign people able to create our own destiny.

What's wrong with America?

Politicians and statesmen trying to impose our will and our form of government on other sovereign nations.

What's right with America?

People — The American people, when left to their own resources, can make a better life for themselves, their families and their communities.

What's wrong with America?

A federal government that thinks it knows more than the American people.

What's right with America?

The United States Constitution!

What's wrong with America?

Politicians who can't understand they are there to serve the American people and to uphold the Constitution of the Unites States of America.

# Chapter 20 **Class Warfare**

Today, In America, we, the people, are divided. Divided amongst ourselves. Today, In America, it's Us versus Them. Rich versus non-rich. Today, in America we, the people, are actively engaged in class warfare. Class warfare based on the great financial divide between the rich and the poor. Between the capitalists and the workers. Between the unions and management. Class warfare. Biting. Hateful. Tearing the country apart. Class warfare in America, politically initiated and promoted and inflamed by the current Democratic White House, Congressional Democrats and the current Democratic President of the United States. Class warfare. Hate and anger and mistrust directed toward the richest 1% of Americans. Class warfare. Based on what? Lies and misinformation.

Let's set the record straight …

From the New York Post, Michael Tanner, Nov 7, 2011: "So just who are those top 1 percent of Americans that we're all supposed to hate? If you listen to President Obama, the protesters at Occupy Wall Street, and much of the media, it's obvious. They're either "trust-fund babies" who inherited their money, or greedy bankers and hedge-fund managers. Certainly, they haven't worked especially hard for their money. While the recession has thrown millions of Americans out of work, they've been getting even richer. Worse, they don't even pay their fair share in taxes: Millionaires and billionaires are paying a lower tax rate than their secretaries.

**In reality, each of these stereotypes is wrong.**
Roughly 80 percent of millionaires in America are the first generation of their family to be rich. They didn't inherit their wealth; they earned it. How? According to a recent survey of the top 1 percent of American earners, slightly less than 14 percent were involved in banking or finance.

Roughly a third were entrepreneurs or managers of non-financial businesses.

Nearly 16 percent were doctors or other medical professionals.

Lawyers made up slightly more than 8 percent, and engineers, scientists and computer professionals another 6.6 percent.

Sports and entertainment figures -- the folks flying in on their private jets to express solidarity with the anti-rich protestors -- composed almost 2 percent.

By and large, the wealthy have worked hard for their money. NYU sociologist Dalton Conley says that "higher-income folks work more hours than lower-wage earners do."
Because so much of their income is tied up in investments, the recession has hit the rich especially hard. Much attention has been paid recently to a Congressional Budget Office study that showed incomes for the top 1 percent rose far faster from 1980 until 2007 than for the rest of us. But the nonpartisan Tax Foundation has found that from … 2007-2010 … there has been a 39 percent decline in the

number of American millionaires.

Among the "super-rich," the decline has been even sharper: The number of Americans earning more than $10 million a year has fallen by 55 percent. In fact, while in 2008 the top 1 percent earned 20 percent of all income here, that figure has declined to just 16 percent. Inequality in America is declining.

As for not paying their fair share, the top 1 percent pay 36.7 percent of all federal income taxes. Because, as noted above, they earn just 16 percent of all income, that certainly seems like more than a fair share. ... Overall, the rich pay an effective tax rate (after all deductions and exemptions) of roughly 24 percent. For all taxpayers as a group, the average effective tax rate is about 11 percent.

Beyond taxes, the rich also pay in terms of private charity. Households with more than $1 million in income donated more than $150 billion to charity last year, roughly half of all US charitable donations. Greedy? It hardly seems so.

And let us not forget the fact that the rich provide the investment capital that funds ventures, creates jobs and spurs innovation. The money that the rich save and invest is the money that companies use to start or expand businesses, buy machinery and other physical capital and hire workers.

It has become fashionable to ridicule the idea of the rich as "job creators," but if the rich don't create jobs, who will? How many workers have been hired recently by the poor?
No doubt dishonest or unscrupulous businessmen have gotten rich by taking advantage of others. And few of us are likely to lose much sleep over the plight of the rich.

But shouldn't public policy be based on something more than class warfare, envy and stereotypes?"

# Chapter 21 **What is America?**

*U.S. Constitution*

In the past 40 years I have seen America change. Change that threw away the fundamentals that created America, threw away the fundamentals that built America, threw away the fundamentals that made America great, threw away the fundamentals that made America, well, America.

America was founded on 2 basic principles. Freedom. And opportunity.

The fundamentals of America used to include:

- self-reliance
- independence
- personal freedom - to succeed or fail
- hard work
- merit pay
- risk taking
- creativity
- majority rules
- money talks bullshit walks

- character
- honesty
- having a clear sense of right and wrong
- emphasis on good basic public education
- basic intelligence
- common sense
- risk vs. reward
- aspiring to a better life, by earning it
- good sound practical ideas

These "old fashioned" traits epitomize Wall Street. With some exceptions, exceptions of bad people doing bad things. The exceptions are, thankfully, not the rule and are rarer than the media reports and the public believes.

Today, we have a new America. An America where a large percentage of the population believes …

- everyone should be the same.
- the individual should be de-emphasized and de-valued and the government should mandate and dictate a citizen's behavior.
- everyone should be given the basics of a good life.
- the government should force everyone to live according to how the government wants you to live, not how YOU as an individual want to live.
- the government should determine your choices; how much water is in your toilet, how many miles per gallon your vehicle must get and what kind of light bulbs you can use.
- not the majority, but a minority of one (1) should set the rules.
- wealth should be taken away from those who took risks and earned it and handed to those who didn't risk and didn't earn it.
- pay should not be based on merit but based on length of time on the job, regardless of work ethic or productivity.
- workers who contribute little or nothing towards creating goods, services and jobs should be paid the same as those who do.

The new America is something else. Literally, something else. The "new" America is not America at all. It's something else. And the new America is not special. It now is starting to resemble all the other civilized (and socialistic) countries, especially those in Europe. And in doing so America will lack true freedom. And true opportunity. Freedom and opportunity. Freedom and opportunity for YOU. And your children and your children's children. Allowed to continue down its new path the new America will take away YOUR freedom and opportunity … the freedom and opportunity to make the life you want and live the life you want.

To those who believe in the new America, a "fairer and nicer" America I say who said life was fair? Who said life was "nice"? Who said life was easy? To those who want everything handed to them, without earning it, without risk, I say "No guts, no glory!"

The big problem is that you cannot combine the best of the "old" America and the best of the "new" America. Because they are fundamentally incompatible. As the future unfolds it's going to be either one or the other. The new "old" America means going forward into the future by going back to the past … and updating the best of the past. The "new" America means going forward into the future by going forward and becoming Europe … and updating the worst of a government-based socialistic society.

Freedom and opportunity versus no freedom and no opportunity. The new "old" America or the new "new" America.

Which America do YOU choose?

# Chapter 22 **Capitalism in Trouble**

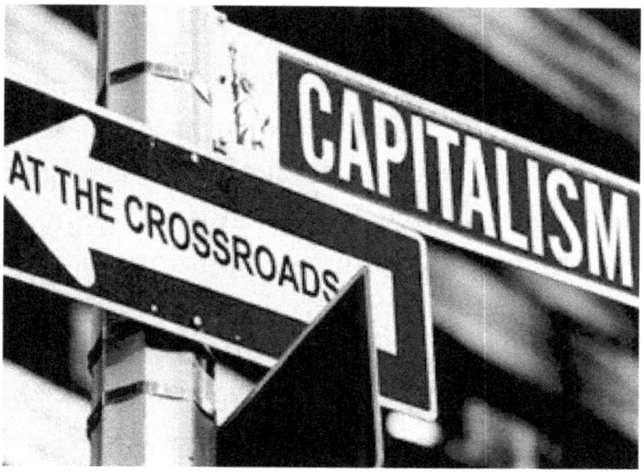


Thursday, April 09, 2009

**Rasmussen Reports: Just 53% Say Capitalism Better Than Socialism …**

"Only 53% of American adults believe capitalism is better than socialism. The latest Rasmussen Reports national telephone survey found that 20% disagree and say socialism is better. Twenty-seven percent (27%) are not sure which is better.

Adults under 30 are essentially evenly divided: 37% prefer capitalism, 33% socialism, and 30% are undecided.

Thirty-somethings are a bit more supportive of the free-enterprise approach with 49% for capitalism and 26% for socialism.

Adults over 40 strongly favor capitalism, and just 13% of those older Americans believe socialism is better …

There is a partisan gap as well. Republicans - by an 11-to-1 margin - favor capitalism. **Democrats are much more closely divided: Just 39% say capitalism is better while 30% prefer socialism"…**

This clearly illustrates that at least 30% of Democrats in 2009 were dangerous to your freedom and opportunity, your future, the future of democracy. 30% of Democrats prefer to change America into socialist America. I would imagine that most of the people in America preferring socialism are among the 40+ million poor, the 18-24-year-olds, government and union workers, and far-left liberals. They no doubt believe that they will be better off under American socialism. They are wrong. What they do not realize is that they will have far fewer choices and far less freedom about how they can live their lives. If America becomes socialist they won't like it. They won't like it one bit. Unfortunately, once the U.S. Constitution and the Bill of Rights is ignored - or thrown away - and government controls many or all aspects of American life, it'll be too late to take back our freedom. YOUR freedom. And YOUR freedom and opportunity, the freedom and opportunity to live your life the way YOU want to live it, will be determined … not by you … but by the government.

American capitalism or American socialism. Which will YOU choose?

The End

## Top 5 Books by Andrew Lawrence

*available at amazon.com*

1. **The Happiness Transformation**
   The Happiness Transformation reveals how to be genuinely happy - NOW - and for the rest of your life.

2. **Discover Your Life Purpose in 30 Minutes**
   An interactive book which quickly reveals your unique and special purpose in life.

3. **MONEY - The Basics**
   An easy to understand book about money. A must-read for anyone who wants to be more money savvy. "The most valuable book you'll ever read".

4. **Stories Of A Lifetime**
   Inspirational true stories of extraordinary events in an extraordinary life. Mine. Amazing and true stories. A motivational masterpiece!

5. **Soul Sex: The Ultimate Pleasure**
   This book provides fascinating and enlightening
   insights into the age old mystery of the soul, and introduces a whole new level of sex - soul sex.

*Free excerpts at: http://Andrew-Lawrence.blogspot.com*

# Free excerpts from “MONEY - The Basics”

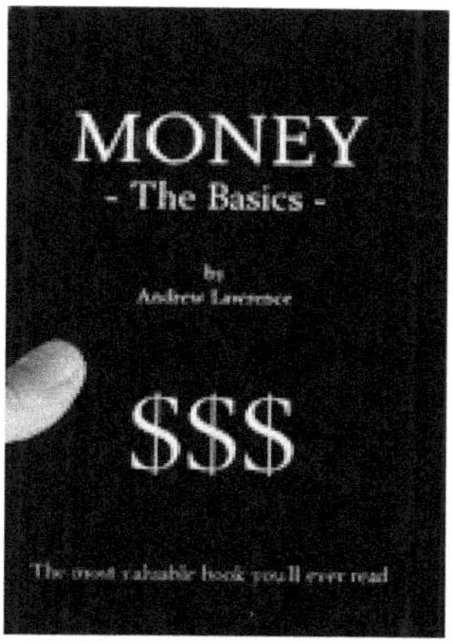


**Introduction**

When it comes to something as important in life as money it is astonishing that so many people understand so little about it.

Whether you are just starting your first job, or are earning minimum wage, or on your way to your first million, or working on your second billion, chances are you don’t know enough about money.

Whether you are an entrepreneur, an employer, an employee, a housewife, a government or union worker, an artist, or retired, chances are you don’t know enough about money.

For the millions of adults in America who would like to have a working knowledge and understanding about the world’s most wanted commodity here is a simple, insightful and entertaining little book containing what you really want, and need, to know about money.

Yes, I know, when it comes to money you just want some. Or want lots of it. Wanting it is not enough.

“MONEY - The Basics”. Read the book. It could be the most important and most valuable book you’ll ever read.

# Chapter 1 **Let There Be Money**

**Genesis**

Back in the day, Adam and Eve's day, there was no money. Money did not exist. Because there was nothing to buy. If you wanted food you picked it off a tree or picked it up from the ground. No one needed money. Because no one bought "things". "Things" hadn't been invented yet.

According to PBS' Nova Online, "The History of Money", in the beginning there was barter. Barter is the exchange of goods and services with mutually agreed upon equal value, i.e., I'll trade you an apple for an orange.

**9,000-6,000 B.C.**

Livestock became the first and oldest form of money. Livestock included cows, sheep, donkeys and camels. With the cultivation of land agricultural products like grain and vegetables became an additional standard form of money.

**1,200 B.C.**

The shell of the mollusk, called a cowrie, was widely found in the Pacific and Indian Oceans. Cowries were first used in China as money twelve hundred years before Christ and was used by many other ancient civilizations. The cowrie is considered to be the longest used form of money in history.

**1,000 B.C.**

Metal money, made of bronze and copper, made its appearance in China at the end of the Stone Age. This metal money could be considered among the earliest versions of metal coins.

**500 B.C.**

Precious metal coins, made from silver and gold, first made their appearance in Lydia (a part of Turkey) in 500 B.C. and were later refined by the Greeks, Persians, Romans and other dominant civilizations.

**100 B.C.**

Leather money was used in China, in the form of 12-inch square decorated deerskin. This leather money could be considered as a forerunner of paper money.

**800 A.D.**

Paper money first appeared in China and was used from 800-1400 A.D. This was many years before paper money was used in Europe and 300 years before paper money was considered a common form of money.

**1800 A.D.**

In 1816 England instituted the Gold Standard. England issued paper money, known as banknotes, that were backed by gold. Gold backed paper money of various major nations continued until the United States went off the Gold Standard and stopped backing the U.S. dollar with gold, in 1971.

**The Present**

Today, paper money and coins in America are no longer backed by precious metals and are based on the "full faith and credit" of the United States of America. Today, currencies "float" and it is the worldwide marketplace and currency traders that determines a currency's value.

# Chapter 3 **Why You Need More Money**

Even if you live in a third-world country you need enough money to live on or to have and maintain a decent standard of living for you and your family. Everything costs money and every year most things cost more than the year before.

In most free societies, like America, the more money you have the more safety, freedom and independence you have.

Money allows you to have choices. With more money you and your family can live in a better neighborhood, your kids can get a better education, you can have a nicer home and have nicer things. And not have to worry so much about your financial situation. With more money you can also help others who are less fortunate.

And if you have lots of money you can be totally independent. And never be the victim of a bad boss, a lousy old car that doesn't run or bills you can't pay. Having money can make your life easier and more enjoyable. That is not to say that money alone will make you happy. You also need good health, good values and a good outlook. But if used wisely money can improve your life. A lot.

Everyone dreams of being rich. Why? Because it is better to be rich than poor. In today's modern and expensive world if you want to have a good life, or build a better one, you need plenty of money.

# Chapter 7 **How To Get Money**

Want to be one of the lucky ones on the road to riches, want to be on the freeway to financial freedom, on your way to wealth?

Here are the top 7 roads to riches, the top 7 easiest and fastest ways to acquire money ...

**Inherit it**

This is how America's old money families got their wealth. In the 1800's and early 1900's, before anti-trust laws, income taxes and political correctness, America's leading families built empires and amassed great wealth; in industries such as oil, banking, newspapers, sugar, transportation, land, and even bootlegging. And that original wealth was passed down to succeeding generations. The number one easiest and fastest way to acquire wealth is to inherit it. Unfortunately, inheriting wealth is mainly a matter of blood; you have to be born into the right family.

**Marry it**

If you can't inherit it the second easiest and fastest way to acquire wealth is to marry someone who is already wealthy. And sometimes that person may even be kind, generous, compatible and loveable. And, if not, divorce can pay off handsomely. Just remember to get married (and divorced) in a state that has favorable community property laws, and watch out for those pre-nuptial agreements.

**Work for it**

If you can't inherit wealth and can't marry it then you can work for it. People rarely get rich having a job. Rather, people who get rich working for a living start a company and build it up. And own the whole thing. And then they often take that company public (sell stock to the public), collecting hundreds of millions, or billions, of dollars in doing so. Or, they invent something useful and valuable which greatly benefits society, such as a better clothes hanger, dynamite, or the paper clip.

**Win it**

If you can't inherit wealth, can't marry it or can't work for it then maybe you can win it. Lotteries abound, paying out multi-million dollar jackpots, and eventually someone always wins them. Unfortunately, you have a greater chance of being struck by lightning then winning the lottery. But, hey, it only costs a buck!

**Steal it or deal it**

If you can't inherit wealth and you can't marry it, work for it, or win it then maybe you could steal it or deal it …

You could become a CEO or chief financial officer for a big cash-rich company, cook the books, steal millions of dollars, buy a $20 million dollar home, lie to the feds, and hope you don't get caught, convicted and sent to prison. I don't recommend anyone try to get rich this way.

Also not recommended is to deal it; to become a drug lord and generate tens of millions of dollars in cash dealing heroin, crack, meth and other non-FDA approved goodies, and wholesaling it to pushers who will gladly resell it to anyone to wants it, ranging from children to movie stars. After all, aren't drug dealers just supplying what people want; even if it creates crime, ruins lives, kills people or could put them in jail for the rest of their life. Not a legal (or moral) way to get rich.

**Gamble for it**

If you can't inherit money, can't marry it, can't work for it, can't win it, can't steal or deal it then maybe you could gamble for it. Over 50 million people play poker. A few even make millions of dollars at it. You've seen them on television, winning or losing upwards of a million dollars on the turn of a card. Looks easy, doesn't it? They don't look so tough on TV; I bet any decent poker player (like me for instance) has a good chance of beating them on a lucky day. So maybe you could simply plunk down $3,000-$25,000 per tournament entry fee, or get a backer, join the World Poker Tour, win a few tournaments and get rich! Or maybe, in reality, the average amateur poker player has a snowball's chance in hell of getting rich that way.

**Invest and get rich**

If you can't inherit wealth, can't marry it, can't work for it, can't win it, can't steal or deal it or can't gamble for it then maybe you can invest and get rich. There are 2 good ways to invest and get rich; the real estate market and the stock market. According to historical data, over time, real estate goes up a average of 10% a year. So getting rich in real estate tends to take a long time. And also requires a large down payment. Hard to get rich quick that way.

On the other hand, the stock market can be a good way to get rich. Stocks can go up dramatically over a relatively short period of time and make you rich but you have to have the money to invest and you have to pick the right stocks at the right time. And stocks can go up in value and they can also go down in value.

To recap how to get rich:

1. inherit it
2. marry it
3. work for it
4. win it
5. steal it or deal it
6. gamble for it
7. invest for it

These are the top 7 easiest and quickest ways people can get rich. How will YOU do it?

*I hope you enjoyed the free excerpts ... and want to read more of the book. "MONEY-The Basics" is available in paperback at amazon. com*

www.ingramcontent.com/pod-product-compliance
Lightning Source LLC
Chambersburg PA
CBHW051326170526
45166CB00002B/701
* 9 7 8 1 4 6 7 9 1 9 5 0 0 *